PRAY THERE BEFORE YOU GET THERE

by

Mary Simpson

Published by

Denver, CO. 80239

Unless otherwise indicated,
all Scripture quotations are taken from
the *King James* Version of the Bible.

Pray There Before You Get There
Copyright © 2008 by Mary Simpson
P.O. Box 39846
Denver, CO 80239

ISBN NO. 9781427630131

Published by Marriage Connection
P.O. Box 39846
Denver, CO. 80239

Printed in the United States of America
All rights reserved under International Copyright Law.
Contents and/or cover may not be reproduced in whole or in part in any form without the express written consent of the Publisher.

Table of Contents

DEDICATION VII

ACKNOWLEDGMENT IX

INTRODUCTION XI

PART I: MAKING THE CUT

CHAPTER 1: WHAT IS PRAYER? 17
Hope or Wish

CHAPTER 2: SIX WAYS TO COMMUNICATE WITH GOD 21
Prayer
Supplications
Intercessions
Groanings
Thanksgivings
Meditations

CHAPTER 3: DOES GOD ACTUALLY ANSWER PRAYERS? 43
The Believer's Theory
The Skeptic's Theory:
    God Does What He Wants to Anyway.
        Doesn't He?

I Do Not Have Enough Time
I Do Not Believe I Will Get What I Ask For
I Will Ask Someone Else to Pray
Everything Will Inevitably Work Out
I'll Make Prayer My Last Resort

**CHAPTER 4: PRAYER OF FAITH—
PRAYER OF FEAR..69**

PART II: GRADUATE TO THE NEXT LEVEL

**CHAPTER 5: JESUS—ELIJAH—
MOSES—JOSHUA..77**
Elijah Prayed and it did Not Rain
Moses Commanded the Waters
Jesus Spoke to the Wind and Waters
The Sun Stood Still and the Moon Stayed

**CHAPTER 6: BELIEVING PRAYER
PULLS DOWN DIVINE AID......................................85**
What Can't He do, Who has Done This?

PART III: WISDOM AND KNOWLEDGE IS KEY

**CHAPTER 7: HOW TO ALWAYS GET
ANSWERS TO YOUR PRAYERS..............................95**
Come Boldly Before the Throne of God

Ask the Father in the Name of Jesus
Ask in Faith Nothing Wavering
Pray the Word of God
Pray God's Will
Pray Fervently
Be Persistent
Worship Him, and Give Praise and Thanks
Forgive Others
Apply Spiritual Authority
Be Precise

CHAPTER 8: NINE REASONS FOR UNANSWERED PRAYER..........123
Lack of Faith
Wrong Reason Wrong Season
Wavering
Not Asking According to God's Will
Sin in One's Life
Ask Amiss
Pure Unadulterated Unbelief
A Prophet is Without Honor
A Need for Prayer and Fasting

CHAPTER 9: AN OPEN LINE FOR PRAYER..........135
- How Long Should We Pray
- A Set Time and Place for Prayer

ABOUT YOUR AUTHOR

Dedication

I was a fairly new Christian when my friend and sister in the Lord, **Coleen Keener,** being newly saved herself, began to call and pray with me for countless hours over the phone. She is a blessed, gifted, and anointed prayer warrior, and as I sat listening to her pray, a deep desire to speak to God as she did was developed down in my spirit. That valuable time we spent praying together ultimately birthed in me an anointing for prayer.

—*T*hanks *C*oleen—

Acknowledgment

With a thankful heart, I hold high regards for all the people who have ever deemed it necessary to intercede for, and pray along with me, at significant times throughout my life. I would not be who I am today, had I not been upon your hearts in those necessitous periods of time.

As a child, my mother prayed for me. As a wife, my husband continually prays for me. As a mother, my children love and pray for me. As a sibling, my other siblings have deemed in a worthy cause to pray for me. As a friend, my friends have made it their choice to pray for me; and as a child of God, many I do not know but will one day have the privilege of thanking, have interceded on my behalf. So if by happenchance any of you are reading this right now, know that I hold heartfelt appreciation for every word you have ever uttered to God on my behalf.

Further recognition is given to my pastor, Alvin Simpkins, who I know to be a man of prayer. I have served under his great tutelage for a number of years and have spent numerous hours, working the prayer line as a prayer warrior. Now serving as one of the ministers for the church he pastors,

(Emmanuel Christian Center) we are masterfully guided in ways of prayer.

Sincere thanks is also given for the work of my copy-editor, Felicia Ransom, whose editing expertise can be found on every page throughout this work.

Introduction

From the foundation of the world, prayer has always been a way for God to commune with His creation. At the beginning, fellowship and communion between Himself and humanity was what God originally planned prayer to be. It was simply Him walking with, talking to, and communing with humans in the cool of the day. This avant-garde way of God communing with humanity was soon to change.

Adam and Eve's sin of disobedience caused a dreadful fall in the Garden of Eden, which precipitated a separation between God and His creation, thereby; ushering in sin and destruction. At that point, prayer went from being direct communion and a simple walk in the cool of the garden, to becoming a need for humans to petition God for intervention on their behalf.

And then men began to call upon the name of the Lord (Gen. 4:26). If the "first humans" would not have taken that horrible fall, then there would not be a need for us to call on God for help in averting evil, because in the Garden, there was no sickness, no disease, no hurt, pain, ruin, or devastation—only harmony between God and His creation.

Nevertheless, because of the "Fall," sin entered the world and became rampant. Humankind—now being weak—became subservient, as sin took over. Along with uncontrolled sin, death entered the world, and brought with it: sickness, disease, wickedness, jealousy, envy, malice, and every evil work. This caused humanity to start functioning in an ailing state of devastation. Because the destruction of humanity had begun—brought about through the act of one man's sin, and the effects it had on our lives—humans no longer basked in the direct presence of God uninhibited; walking through the paradisaic garden as they talked with Him in the cool of the day. Instead, restraints were put into place, and a need arose for prayer to be done in a different way. Humans still enter the presence of God and commune with Him through prayers of adoration, but added to that communion are: pleas, petitions, intercessions and supplications, requesting God's help to keep them from sliding deeper into the clutches of sin.

God has made it a requirement that Christians pray. In Ezekiel 22:30, God says that He looked for someone to stand in the gap before Him and the land so that He would not bring about destruction to it, but He did not find *one*.

The ministry of Prayer in today's church, is somewhat of a forgotten piece of the big puzzle of church organization. The prosperity of any ministry hinges on prayer, so why are there so few members interested in it? Number one, it is a thankless job, which is done primarily in secret and is not a sinecure. Secondly, a common thread throughout main stream Christendom is the belief that most of their prayers are not answered anyway. God said His house shall be called a house of prayer (Isa. 56:7), so how did we as watchmen on the wall, manage to let that mindset take a stronghold and become so prevalent in this Christian era?

Can anyone pray to God? Will He answer them? Are there prayers that can move the hand of God while others fall flat? Prayer is the only means by which we communicate with our father, so there is a need for us to understand how. Now let us turn the page as we explore.

CUT

Part I

Making the CUT

Can and will Prayer work for you.

Understanding what Prayer is.

The how's, when's, and where's, of Prayer.

*"Always send the Word of God

to a situation or place

before you arrive there."*
—*Mary Simpson*—

Chapter 1

What Is Prayer?

Prayer is the most powerful tool in the universe. It can take you places no other specified mode of transportation can or will. As humans, we have found that the speed of light is the fastest any object can travel, but prayer moves even faster than that. We know this assertion to be true, because there is no distance in prayer, being that we pray to an omnipresent God who is everywhere at the same time. With the far reaching capabilities that prayer has, it is the fastest carrier that can get help to a place, or situation before your physical body can arrive.

Aircraft carriers must wait for permission from an air traffic controller in order to take flight, but prayer only has to be released from your spirit and it can get to the place you send it faster than the Concorde. You must *Pray There Before you Get There*. Always send the Word of God to a place or situation in advance of your arrival.

What is prayer? A lot of people think they know what prayer is, but do they really? The term, prayer, when used by Christians, is defined as: "Communication with the all-knowing, all-powerful, true and living God of this universe. It is a spoken, or unspoken exchange of information with God in the form of thanksgivings, expressions of praise, confession, or even an earnest request made from the sincere desires of one's heart. It is a petition made in faith unto God, **knowing**—not just believing, but knowing past believing; deep down in your innermost being—that He hears and will answer you, because His Word says so."

> *"And if we know that He [hears] us,*
> *whatsoever we ask,*
> *we know that we have*
> *the petitions that we desired of Him."*
> 1 John 5:15

Hope or Wish

In order for us not to just surmise, but totally comprehend what prayer is, it would be beneficial for us to know what prayer is "NOT."

Petitionary prayer is not simply a "hope" or a "wish." It is not, "I might get what I want, if I hope or wish for it long and hard enough." It is a sincere release of God's Word back to Him in the form of a request.

While in the course of making our requests known, we must release our faith, believing that He will grasp hold of our petitions and not let them go unanswered. In Isaiah 55:11, God said that His Word *will not* return unto Him void, but would accomplish that which He pleases and would prosper in the thing where unto He sends it. "Believing Prayer" is being fully persuaded and possessing no doubt, that the words from Scripture which are released from your mouth, will produce a desired result.

God places His Word even above His name. He is God of His Word. If He said it, He will do it, and if He spoke it, He is faithful to bring it to pass. We get answers to prayer by *praying the answer* we are seeking, in accordance with God's Word. God moves on a situation *only* when His Word is spoken over it. So in order to pray earth-shaking prayers, one must first find out from the Word of God, what His promises are concerning their specific set of circumstances. To be prepared to pray God's Word, one must know it. So to that we say as Paul said to Timothy; *"Study to shew thyself approved unto God, a workman that needeth not to be ashamed, rightly dividing the Word of truth"* (2 Tim. 2:15).

God, in His zealousness to help facilitate us in getting the answers we are seeking after, gave us benefits in the form of ministering angels. When they launch out to bring back help, it is only on the spoken Word of God that they take flight. When someone prays and does not choose to use the Word of God, they *are* simply making use of their native language by calling out words; or they deliver some elaborate dissertation, which will more than likely reverberate off the walls. Therefore, we must make sure we pray God's Word and not just hope, or wish.

Chapter 2

Six Ways We Communicate With God

When we enter the presence of God to begin communion with Him, we cross the threshold in six different ways. As we approach, we come by way of prayers, supplications, intercessions, groanings, thanksgivings and meditations. We must first come before God with our heart filled with love, honor, and respect. Our body should be ready to lift up holy hands, kneel at His feet, or even lay prostrate on the floor, while our spirit is getting ready to receive revelation and wisdom from His life-giving Word.

"I exhort therefore, that, first of all, supplications, prayers, intercessions, and giving of thanks, be made for all men."

1 Tim. 2:1

"Be careful for nothing; but in [everything] by prayer and supplication with thanksgiving let your requests be made known unto God."

Phil. 4:6

Prayer

When we enter the presence of God by way of prayer, we do so in order to obtain things. "Give me, lend me, let me have," is a more witty turn of phrase. Prayers made by individuals are, for the most part, personal. They ask God for help, they bargain with Him, make pleas unto Him, they adjure and implore, while begging and making emphatic statements of appeal to Him. They make claims as they complain, petition and beseech Him. Then they make demands and assertions, while on the other hand they declare and they decree. They make allegations, they deny, they agree, they refuse, they proclaim, they lobby, then finally, they just say,

"YES LORD!"

There are eight types of prayers we find listed in Scripture that are regarded by God:

Prayer of faith..................................James 5:15

Elder's prayer..................................James 5:14

Prayer of the destitute....................Psalms 102:17

Servant's prayer.................................Kings 8:28

Prayer of the afflicted.......................Psalms 102:1

Prayer of the people (Corporate)..........Psalms 80:4

Prayer of the righteous..................Proverbs 15:29

The Lord's Prayer ....Matthew 6:9-13

All of the above prayers are made in accordance with the Word of God.

With the **"prayer of faith"** we lay out our petitions before God, and we make our request known unto Him. In conjunction with that, we employ faith, because without faith we will not obtain anything from God.

The **"elder's prayer"** is prayed when there are those who are sick in the congregation. They are brought forth, and as the elders lay hands on them, they *will* be healed.

The **"prayer of the destitute"** will not be despised by the Lord. His ears are open unto their cry. He does not discard them because of the condition they find themselves in. The people we would more than likely pass on the street and never take a glance at—and most assuredly not a second look, or give further thought to—God will look upon. Men despise men, but the Word of God asks this question, *"But whoso hath this world's good, and seeth his brother have need, and [shuts] up his bowels of compassion from him, how dwelleth the love of God in him"* (1 John 3:17)? There are two hundred-five references to "poor" found in Scripture; so we know, by sheer numbers alone, the poor and destitute are wholly on the heart of God.

It is my heartfelt belief that God holds the **"servant's prayer"** with such regard because it is His desire that we all become servants, and live the life of a servant. While Jesus was here on earth pursuing His ministry, He took on the form of a servant, and it is God's desire that we be like-minded.

"Let this mind be in you, which was also in Christ Jesus: Who, being in the form of God, thought it not robbery to be equal with God: But made himself of no reputation, and took upon Him the form of a servant, and was made in the likeness of men: and being found in fashion as a man, He humbled himself, and became obedient unto death, even the death of the cross."

Phil. 2:5-8

Ministry in itself is servanthood. *"For we preach not ourselves, but Christ Jesus the Lord; and ourselves your servants for Jesus' sake"* (2 Cor. 4:5). We are all ministers, and as we render service to others, God considers our prayers. He is not unrighteous to forget our work and labor of love in that we have ministered to the saints (Heb. 6:10).

Jesus showed the greatest example of service, and humility when He washed the feet of His disciples. If we do not walk in humility we cannot be followers of Christ. Scripture says that pride comes before destruction and a haughty spirit goes before a fall (Prov. 16:18), and in 1 Peter 5:5-6, God informs us that He resists the proud, and giveth grace to the humble. That is the reason we must humble ourselves therefore under the mighty hand of God, so He may exalt us in due time (1 Peter 5:6).

Psalms 102 is entitled, **"The prayer of the afflicted,"** and is also known as the prayer of the "the sufferer." This prayer is considered by God because it is not necessarily the prayer of a sinner, but rather the prayer of a person who is enduring a great amount of suffering. Scripture says in 1 Peter 3:14, that we do not only suffer because of sin, but there are times in which we also suffer for righteousness sake. When one is afflicted, they are overwhelmed, distressed, aggrieved, tormented, and even hurt. Once they get tired of being sick and tired of that state of being, they begin to pour out their heart before God, and He gladly lends an ear unto their cries.

The **"prayers of the people"** are heard by God because in Scripture He declares that if two or three are gathered in His name, He would find His place in the midst of them; and if God makes His presence known anywhere, He brings along with Him power for the hour. Corporate prayer is made when the children of God come together in power and unity. Because there is great power in the prayer of agreement—one being able to chase a thousand demons, and two being able to put ten times that many to flight (Deut. 32:30)—God instructs us not to forget to assemble ourselves together and unite.

> *"The power of numbers*
> *is only made more powerful,*
> *by the spirit of unity."*
> —Mary Simpson—

The **"prayer of the righteous"** God will not reject. Scripture definitely makes it known that God does not hear sinners, but if a person walks in obedience to His Word, God will open His ears to hear them, whenever they call out to Him. Proverbs 15:29 lets us know that, *"The LORD is far from the wicked: but He heareth the prayer of the righteous."* For they cry and the Lord hears them, and delivers them out of all of their troubles (Ps. 34:17).

The Lord's Prayer:
There was something so unique, powerful, and amazing about the way Jesus prayed, that it arrested the attention of His disciples. In Luke 11:1, the disciples asked Jesus if He would teach them how to pray. Matthew 6:9-13 holds the words Jesus gave to His disciples in the form of a model prayer; which we have come to know as,

"The Lords' Prayer."

He instructed them, *"after this manner therefore pray ye:*
Our Father which art in heaven, hallowed be Thy name. Thy kingdom come. Thy will be done in earth, as it is in heaven. Give us this day our daily bread. And forgive us our debts, as we forgive our debtors. And lead us not into temptation, but deliver us from evil: for thine is the kingdom, and the power, and the glory, [forever]. Amen"

We should receive the model Jesus laid out, teaching us how to pray, as good advice; and then extrapolate from it. This prayer is the foundation and framework we build and personalize our prayers around. Now let's make note of how the Lord's Prayer breaks down, and how it can be synthesized with the "personal petitions" we bring before God.

We must never approach the throne of God without first acknowledging, God as being God. When we say, **"Our Father,"** we are recognizing Him not just as father of all, but "our" Father and we are His blood-bought children.

Next when we pray, **"which art in heaven,"** we're proclaiming that God is not our earthly father, but we are priding ourselves in the fact that He is our heavenly Father. We are declaring that our esteem and significance is no longer found in who our daddy is; but we have been born again, and who we are now, is establish in our heavenly Father—whose throne is in Heaven.

When we pray, **"hallowed be Thy name,"** we use this adjective to describe God, because He did not just start being God, but from the beginning, He *is* God. He is the *First and the Last*. He is the *Alpha and the Omega—the Beginning and the Ending*. With reverence, we esteem Him supreme, and we hallow His name as we declare there is none like Him either in Heaven or on earth. As His children, we should never approach our Father and begin asking for things without first offering up praise to Him, because in the midst of praise is where we capture His attention.

As we move on to pray, **"Thy Kingdom come,"** we're asking God to let the *good news* of the Gospel, which we have been blessed to receive, be preached to everyone; not just me, my four, and no more, but it is our desire that the Good News be preached even to the youngest baby in the most remote place on earth.

Next our desire is, ***"Thy will be done in earth, as it is in heaven."*** In so doing, we are praying for the majesty of Heaven to come down and manifest in our earthly realm. In that instance, we would have in this world, a measure of the peace, joy, and love that abides in Heaven; thereby making our experience here on earth, a little piece of heaven. We are also praying that the good pleasure of God's will for us be done; and that our will would be superseded by His will, or that our desires would mesh into His desires for us—as they align and become one. When all of those events come together; He will then give us the desires of our heart, which is ultimately His will for us. If we first seek the kingdom of God and His righteousness, (His will) all the other things we need will be given to us (Eph. 1:9).

Then we can pray, ***"Give us this day our daily bread."*** It is imperative that we pray daily for our spiritual, as well as our natural bread. We find it hard to go a day without natural food, so we should not attempt go a day without spiritual food, which is received as we pray and commune with God. In praying, *"give us this day our daily bread"* we are showing our total reliance and trust in a God who owns everything, and He holds all power and authority needed to give to us that which is needed for our life. At this point in our prayer, we make petitions, not just for bread but, for everything else we stand in need of.

"And forgive us our debts, as we forgive our debtors," should be our plea to God after we have asked for our daily bread. We rely on His forgiveness, because if we regard sin and iniquity in our heart, He will not hear us. And if we do not forgive those who have wronged us, our heavenly Father will not forgive us our sins. Since He previously absolved us, and continues to daily forgive us, we must find it in our hearts to forgive others likewise. If we desire mercy we must first show mercy.

"And lead us not into temptation," should be our next plea, as we rely on the Holy Spirit to keep us from sin, while we are endeavoring to resist Satan and his tactics. **"But deliver us from evil,"** is also our desire, because we do not want to be a stumbling block, or a hindrance to our brother or sister.

From the fall in the Garden, sin has been egregious, and we must be dependant upon the spirit of God to keep us as we go through this life, where there are temptations on every side. God also said that He would not let us be tempted above what we are able to bare, but would instead offer us a way of escape (1Cor. 10:13).

We begin the conclusion of our prayer with reverence to God in somewhat of the same manner we opened it. **"For Thine is the kingdom,"** and everything, both in Heaven and earth, belongs to you, God.

We close by offering up praise and thanksgiving to His name. **"And the power and the glory,"** we realize **"forever,"** belongs to You and You alone, for the great and mighty things You have done! **"Amen,"** and so be it.

Prayer Posture:

The Bible makes reference to five different postures we can position ourselves in as we pray. These selected positions are not listed to infer that they are the only postures we are to pray in, but these are examples of how the men and women of the Bible positioned themselves as they prayed unto God. In so posturing ourselves, we show reverence to the God who is much greater than we are.

> 1. Standing ....Nehemiah 9:5
>
> 2. Kneeling ....Ezra 9:5
>
> 3. Sitting....................1Chronicles 17:6-27
>
> 4. Bowing............................Exodus 34:8
>
> 5. Hands lifted up.................1Timothy 2:8

Supplications

*I*t has been a belief of many, that prayers and supplications are one and the same; but I, along with others, find that there is a distinction, without being a difference. Supplications are the earnest, affectionate, and *continued* application to God for the blessings requested from Him by prayer. "Prayer asks; while supplication expostulates, entreats, urges and re-urges the petition" (Adam Clarke's Commentary). We are advised not to stop before we get the answers we are seeking, but to continue in supplications, as we may at times entreat God for His will, by urging and re-urging Him. Other times we disagree with God's will, and then finally accept His will, as we stand determined not to let Him go until He blesses us (Gen. 32:26). Supplications are made for averting evil. They stop the evil that Satan has aimed at us, and keeps it from prospering.

Intercessions

*I*ntercessions are made on behalf of others. It is God's heart to see us get past "give me, lend me, let me have" and move on to the position of being able to pray on behalf of others. As we grow past personal prayer and move on into greater levels of communicating with God; we should by then possess the faith and authority to pray for the whole world, as well as lay hands on the sick, and see them healed. We should be able to speak to problems and see them resolved, and even decree a thing and consider it established unto us. The world is longing and watching in anticipation for the manifestation of the sons of God, so let's get busy and grow to maturity, because the world needs our voices in the area of prayer.

Prayer is nothing to be dealt with lightly, it is

the "instrument" God has given Christians in order to deter, dismantle, and ultimately destroy the works of darkness. In His genius; God has created a network of believers, which He has strategically placed in all four corners of the universe. At His prompting they will begin calling out to Him on behalf of others. I have heard mighty men and women of God talk valiantly about being in such a state of heavy oppression—not possession, but oppression—by the enemy, until they could not muster up enough strength to pray for themselves. So at that point, with what little strength they had left, they strained out these words to God, "Father, let *somebody* pray for me." At that point, God begins to tap into the wealth of prayer authority He has amassed throughout the earth. He then places that desperate person upon the heart of one, or maybe several intercessors and they are immediately impressed to begin praying. As God dials in, interrupting the sequence of their tranquility, someone answers the call; picks up the line and begins to pray to the Father regarding the needs of that distressed individual. I have heard amazing stories by other intercessors who have said that God brings people before them that are in different countries like Africa, Asia, Europe, etc., and they feel a persuasive urge to begin interceding on their behalf.

Intercession goes on in one form or another, 24 hours a day, seven days a week, and anyone can intercede for someone else. But in order to be a true intercessor, one *must* be called and anointed to function in that calling; because the demands of that call are so much more than the average Christian is willing to obligate themselves to. Some intercessors who are truly called to this ministry, can pray for hours on end, and even days at a time, and they must be "on call" at all times.

As Christians, we should never feel that there is no one who is interceding on our behalf. We can find comfort in the fact that *somebody* is always praying for us. Scripture brings this to light by informing us that Jesus is seated at the right hand of the Father and He is *ever* making intercessions for the saints (Rom. 8:34).

Listed below we find times noted in Scripture of divine outreach, where the people of God interceded on behalf of other individuals or even other cities. When the men and women of God began to intercede, God moved and brought about the much desired provisions they stood in need of.

> A. Abraham interceded for Sodom (Genesis 18:20-33).
> B. Paul interceded for the Ephesians (Ephesians 3: 14-20), Colossians (Colossians 1:9-17) and Philippians (Philippians 1:9-11).
> C. Jesus interceded for His disciples (John 17:6-26).
> D. Moses interceded on behalf of Israel (Exodus 32:11-13; 32:31-32).
> E. Elijah interceded on behalf of the people (1 Kings 18:36-37).

Groanings

*G*roanings are made by the Spirit of God. There are literally times when an individual can be so burdened down until they are incapable of articulating from their mouth or spirit in their native language. In that case, the Spirit takes over to intercede on their behalf, in the form of groanings which cannot be spoken.

My testimony on groanings:

A few years back, my family and I were going through this tremendous time of preparedness (which I will speak in more detail about in other testimonies, as we move further along in this work). God had ordained this time in our lives. Day by day things were getting harder and harder for us—in the natural. I can remember on this one particular day, it seemed like our situation had hit rock bottom. Things were so tough; all we could see was darkness on every side. Because the memory of that moment is seared into my consciousness; I can still today—many years later—see as if it was yesterday, me lying upon the bed, unable to lift my head off the pillow because my burdens were weighing so heavily upon me. I tried to pray, but found myself inarticulate. No words would come out of my mouth. All I could hear were these groans coming up out of my spirit. After laying there for a while; the Spirit of God began to speak to my spirit, letting me know that what I was experiencing was what the Scripture called "groanings." He urged me to take courage. God brought comfort to me at that moment of anguish, by assuring me I was not destitute and unprotected; but was yet being covered in prayer, because the Spirit of God had taken the reigns and was, at that time, praying on my behalf. "In my stead, the Spirit of God had dictated our requests, indited [written] my petitions and drew up my plea, then presented them before the throne of God." (Matthew Henry Commentary)

"Likewise the Spirit also helps in our weaknesses. For we do not know what we should pray for as we ought, but the Spirit Himself makes intercession for us with groanings which cannot be uttered. Now He who searches the hearts knows what the mind of the Spirit is, because He makes intercession for the saints according to the will of God." (NKJV)

Rom. 8:26-27

Thanksgivings

Thanksgivings are given for mercies already received. The Word of God says in 1 Thess. 5:18 that we should, *"In every thing give thanks: for this is the will of God in Christ Jesus concerning [us]."* How could anyone forget to go back and give thanks to God after He so graciously answers their prayers, which beforehand were laid at the foot of His throne? Knowing that we are incapable of doing anything without God's help, we should not walk, but run to Him with thanksgiving upon our lips when He honors His promises to us. Simple politeness says that thanks should be rendered unto the giver of any gift.

So Jesus answered and said, "Were there not ten cleansed? But where are the nine? Were there not any found who returned to give glory to God except this foreigner?" (NKJV)

Luke 17:17-18

"O give thanks unto the LORD; for He is good: for His mercy endureth [forever]."

Ps. 118:29

As we pray God's Word back to Him, we must never forget to begin with thanks. "Father, I thank You that your Word says, 'Healing is the childrens' bread,' and I am your child, so according to your promise, I receive my healing right now. Father I thank You that your Word says, 'I am the head and not the tail, I am above and not beneath,' so pursuant to your Word, I will cease being least. Father I thank You that your Word says, 'You have begun a good work in me and will complete it,' so I am fully persuaded that You will keep my life, as I have entrusted it into your hands. Father I praise

You for your faithfulness to your Word as You watch over it to perform it. I bless your name that there are over 2000 promises in Holy Scripture, which covers every situation I could (with or without cause) find myself in. Thank You!"

Meditations

To meditate is: to imagine, to ponder, to sing, utter and mutter, to devise, to muse, to plan, speak, and even to complain—as we communicate with God regarding His Word. In meditation, one does not ask God for anything *per se*, but what they do is begin to see, through their mind's eye, the Word of God as it is activated and becomes *rhema* in their life. They imagine themselves being what the Word says they are. They mutter the Word over and over until it becomes a part of their spirit. They plan and devise ways of becoming what the Word declares they are. Faith comes by hearing and hearing, again and again the Word of God, over and over, until it becomes a part of you (Rom. 10:17. They sing the Word, they utter the Word, and they envision it transforming their life. If one is not able to visualize what they want, it will never materialize. You have to see it to be it.

> *"This book of the law shall not depart out of thy mouth; but thou shalt meditate therein day and night, that thou mayest observe to do according to all that is written therein: for then thou shalt make thy way prosperous, and then thou shalt have good success."*
>
> Josh. 1:8

In meditation we get to know the heart of God, and His will is always found in His heart.

Chapter

3

Does God Actually Answer Prayers?

THE BELIEVER'S THEORY:

"The Lord is not slack concerning His promises, as some men count slackness;" (2 Peter 3:9).

If He spoke it, He will do it. If He said it, He will bring it to pass. As believers, we must grow to trust God and His Word. We shouldn't wait to find ourselves in the middle of a bad situation and then wonder whether we can trust God or not. We must hold assurance of His trustworthiness well beforehand. When the enemy comes in like a flood, we must *know* that Scripture says God will lift up a standard against him (Isa. 59:19). The Holy Spirit is our standard-bearer, and He will unleash the first blow, in an effort to halt Satan in his tracks, and stop the onslaught of his devastation and destruction.

When we look at the word, flood, it awakens our thoughts to the fact that water is the most powerful force in the universe. When it's raging toward you, to say it would be a wise thing to seek higher ground is an understatement—because along with the waters of a flood comes great destruction. As it rolls forcefully along, it wipes out everything in its path.

When the enemy makes up his mind to inundate us, he attacks in somewhat of the same fashion as a natural flood. He is not playing around; he is a destroyer—that is one of his names. When he starts his torrent, it's intense, violent, strong, furious and rampant, building strength every step of the way, therefore; as believers we must seek higher ground in God, as we elevate our thoughts on His Word. We must possess an indomitable spirit, standing sure, and knowing without any shadow, or doubt, that God hears us and will answer our every plea.

THE FIRM ESTABLISHMENT A BELIEVER STANDS ON:

As a believer:
> I need to know, when I call out to God in the middle of the night, He hears me.

As a promise-receiving believer:
> I need to know, when my child is burning up with a fever of 104° or more, He hears me.

As a favor-attracting believer:
> I need to know, when I am handed a pink slip by my employer, and find myself in search of another job, He hears me.

As an entrepreneurial believer:
> I need to know, when cash is low and payroll is due, He hears me.

As a pardoned believer:
> I need to know, if I have committed a sin, for which I need to be forgiven, He hears me.

As an anointed believer:
> I need to know, when I am down to my last dollar, and need food on my table, He hears me.

As a success-driven believer:
> I need to know, when I am held back on my job, for no apparent reason, He hears me.

As an amour-wearing believer:
> I need to know, when the arrows of fear are launched against me, He hears me.

As a Word-filled believer:
> I need to know, when I am about to plow into the back end of an eighteen-wheeler, and all I have time to say is JESUS, He hears me.

As a blood-washed believer:
> I need to know, when my body is racking with pain, and the doctors say there is nothing more they can do, He hears me.

When our God brings deliverance to us, it is not by the power of one, or the might of many, but it is by His Spirit; which is our standard-bearer.

> *"We go from
> test to test and trial to trial,
> in order to grow from
> faith to faith."*
> —Mary Simpson—

As we grow from "infant faith" to "grown-up faith;" we will eventually get to the point of *knowing*, without any doubt, that God hears and answers our every plea.

THE SKEPTIC'S THEORY:

Why should I pray? God is going to do what He wants to do anyway.

For those who do not want to pray, they can come up with a myriad of reasons why they shouldn't.

Their original and most used excuse is:

God Does What He Wants to Anyway, Doesn't He?

*T*oo often the case, this has been the belief of a lot of humans throughout history. The answer to the question is: "No He does not!" Yes God possesses all power, and any powers that exist are ordained of Him, but He has to be invited in to take care of that which is needed in this earthly realm. We pray because God required it of us. If God's people, who are called by His name, would humble themselves and pray, then would He move on their behalf (2 Chron. 7:14).

From the moment sin entered the world and Satan became the ruler of the earth's atmosphere, bringing with him every evil work, there has been a need for prayer. The reason we pray is because prayer invites God into the middle of our circumstances as we request His help for this world's situations and even our own personal cares. Prayer opens the door for God to come in with all the artillery that Heaven has to offer, and catapult every difficult situation that surrounds us.

I often hear people who hold little or no knowledge of God, or how He operates say, "If God is God why doesn't He do something about the tragedies in the world? Why did He allow such a horrible thing to happen to that innocent little child,' or they may ask, 'Why did God let him, or her die, they were so good?" They may even find it poignant to ask, "Where was God when that natural disaster happened?" My response to them is, "As long as we live in a sinful world, the Word of God declares that it will rain on the just as well as the unjust; therefore, life happens."

Scripture states that there will be earthquakes in divers places as well as wars and rumors of wars (Mark 13:7-8), but God still sits upon the throne. If we ventured to pray and invite God into the middle of our situations, many—but not all—of the things we experience could be averted. If we find that we are praying about some of these things and are not getting answers to our prayers, it could most likely be because of sin in our lives. It is sin that separates us from God, and while we indulge in sin, we are unable to place our request before Him and have Him answer them. *"Behold, the LORD's hand is not shortened, that it cannot save; neither His ear heavy, that it cannot hear: but your iniquities have separated between you and your God, and your sins have hid His face from you, that He will not hear"* (Isa. 59:1-2).

One thing the inquisitive people of the world who ask these types of questions, or make these sort of statements do not realize is; Satan is the ruler of this earth's atmosphere, and he goes about seeking whom he might devour. God has to be invited in to take care of any unfavorable circumstance (Eph. 2:2). I have often heard my pastor (Alvin Simpkins) say, "Heaven waits on earth. Somebody must be praying. If somebody does not pray, someone else will pay." My assertion is, "Prayer invites God in with all of Heaven's weaponry to make right every wrong, and to take care of the situation at hand."

> *Jesus, who is the only*
> *begotten son of God*
> *had to pray,*
> *so why not*
> *the church world.*

I Do Not Have Enough Time

It is not a matter of time, but a matter of heart. If someone has the heart for prayer, they will find the time. Prayer does not always have to be this long, drawn-out ceremonial event. I personally believe that if one goes to God in sincerity, they can pray just as effectively in one minute as they can in one hour. On the other hand, I do realize that a need can arise for extended time in prayer; if on certain occasions one has a great number of petitions to ask of God, or they are awaiting an answer from Him, or while worshiping Him, they may just desire to linger and bask in His presence.

I believe tremendous heartfelt prayer is often found in brevity. The shortest prayer found in Scripture consisted of three words. In Matthew 14:30 after Peter walked out on the water toward Jesus, and then shortly thereafter began to sink, he prayed, "Lord save me!" A lot of laconic prayers we find in Scripture were less than five minutes, so do not feel guilty if you can't pray for hours on end. *"But when ye pray, use not vain repetitions, as the heathen do: for they think that they shall be heard for their much speaking"* (Matt. 6:7).

When in public, the prayers Jesus prayed were

quite short, whereas in private they were much longer. Jesus prayed all night before He gave the "Sermon on the Mount." The longest public prayer He prayed was noted in the 17th chapter of John and was about four or five minutes long.

Do not feel the need to kill time by adding unnecessary flowery words, just pray from the earnestness of your heart and God will hear you. The effectiveness of your prayer is not measured by the hands on a timepiece. However, I will admonish you not to let the above words be justification for not praying longer, when there is a need for a protracted amount of time spent in His presence while praying.

"You may pray for an hour and still not pray. You may meet God for a moment and then be in touch with Him all day."
—Fredrik Wisloff—

I Do Not Believe I Will Get What I Ask For

My time is valuable. Is "prayer time" just a religious exercise in futility, or do my prayers matter? Some people actually do not believe they get answers to their prayers at all. When the term: "I do not have a prayer in '____' of getting what I am asking for" is used, it denotes that the one doing the asking believes that the term "answered prayer" is a nonentity—not existing in the real world. Others believe that "answered prayer" is contingent; supposing that it is possible—but not certain to happen, and if it does happen it is by chance or luck that it does.

How does one get to this frame of mind? Why pray if you do not believe that God hears you and will provide an answer that will change your situation for the better? It is my belief that people possess this mentality because of ignorance concerning God's Word, and what it says about: how to pray, what to pray, when to pray, where to pray, why and to whom we pray. Once this knowledge is gained, I believe "prayer time" will no longer be an occasion one counts down to with apathy, but would become an event looked forward to with much excitement, realizing that this is the time to come face to face with the God of the universe, as He lends an ear to their cry.

> *"Prayer should never be forced, because 'Coerced Prayer' is simply blowing Hot Air"*
> —Mary Simpson—

I Will Ask Someone Else to Pray for Me

"I believe they are closer to God than I am, so I will ask them to pray for me." It is not the other person; it is that person's faith which produces answers to prayer. Faith comes by hearing, and hearing comes by the Word of God (Rom. 10:17). Once an individual gets the Word of God down on the inside, they then possess the faith needed to move the hand of God. His Word says, *"...without faith it is impossible to please Him: for he that cometh to God must believe that He is, and that He is a rewarder of them that diligently seek Him"* (Heb. 11:6).

We cannot say that there is never an occasion when one should ask someone else to pray for them; because Scripture does say if there are any who are sick in a particular congregation that the elders of that church should be called, and they should lay hands on whoever is ill (James 5:14). That being said, there should be no inference drawn from this, purporting that on every occasion in which a need arises, someone else should be called. Just because someone holds a title does not mean they will necessarily have the faith that is needed for your situation. My advice to the person that would make the above unadvised statement is, "Each person, at the end of the day, is responsible for their own soul." One should build up enough "personal faith" to be able to *know* that God hears them. For everyone who *knows* that God hears them when they pray, there has to be a point of reference they can look back to and say, "Because of *this*, I know without any shadow or doubt that God hears me when I pray."

"How can I know if God hears me when I pray?"

This has been an age-old question asked by many since the beginning of time.

My testimony:

The first time I was assured of the fact that God heard me was a few years back when my family and I were going through that time of preparedness I wrote in brief about earlier on in this work. As Charles Dickens' famous quote goes, "It was the best of times, it was the worst of times." We were going through this tug-of-war between what our souls desired and our spirits needed. This requisite time in our lives encompassed a season where things got so tough in the natural, until our soul's desires began decreasing, while at the same time our spirits were growing to a level of such paramount faith in God, until everything we were suffering in the natural, held no comparison to the heights we were being propelled to in our spirits.

During this time, we had to believe God for our natural daily bread. Before your subconscious mind automatically drifts to the most likely train of thought, by reading the white spaces in between the black letters, let me arrest your attention and direct your thoughts back to the correct account of what happened. We were not lazy people. We did not just lie around not working or taking care of our affairs. My husband and I were both college graduates and were doing well in our careers. We owned a house, two cars as well as a plethora of other things, and life was what we considered good, UNTIL: the plans we held for our lives were placed on hold as the plans God held, began to take precedence over ours.

We became subject to the usual vicissitudes that people, who are being prepared to be used by God for His glory, experience. Our lives began this downward spiral as my husband quit his primary job and went back to school desiring a change of career. Contemporaneously and unexpectedly I was handed a pink slip by my employer. Incidentally during that same year, my husband was involved in a car accident in which one of his legs was almost completely severed, and that precipitated him being in bed for the better part of one year.

What's more astonishing, is during that same period of time, God instructed me not to go back to work. (Naturally unbelievable, but He did.) Yes, I know; this conundrum left me baffled also, being that we had three little children to care for.

Things had eventually gotten so tough until, with arrogant ambition, I decided to ignore God's will as I began to say, "I don't have to go through this and allow my kids to endure this epic amount of suffering. I have a degree, I am ingenious and enterprising, I am marketable, and I can get a job." Look at the number of "I's" used in that prideful statement. What a mistake! As I picked up the newspaper and began looking for a job, I heard this emphatic voice, which I recognized immediately as the voice of God, began to speak to me. The words were so resounding in my spirit until; they still rest fresh upon my mind—this many years later. He spoke, "If you want what I want for you, you had better get out of that paper, and do what I told you to do." I flung that paper down as if it was taboo, while saying, "Not my agenda Lord, but yours." I did not pick up another job section of the newspaper until that time of trial and testing was over in our lives. *"A man's heart [devises] his way: but the LORD [directs] his steps"* (Prov. 16:9).

There is nothing wrong with having ambitious goals and desires, as well as the ingenuity and determination to work for them. One of the definitions of ambition is: "to work." In any other normal circumstance, having the grandeur of "ambitions of work" dancing around in my head would have been OK, but there is a time and a season for everything under the sun, and this was not the time or the season for the pursuit of my life's goals.

As God spoke to me in that manner, it was not His designed purpose to break my will for pursuing after *life* and attaining things in it; but His desire was to have my mind renewed so I would begin to want the same things for my life that He desired, being that He holds my best interest at heart and knows the thoughts He has for me to bring me peace and not evil all the days of my life (Jer. 29:11). It was still imperative that I have ambitions in life, but what I needed along with those ambitions was a desire to swap my natural thinking concerning my aspirations, and began to think more spiritually minded.

As I alluded to earlier, on most occasions we did not know where our next meal was coming from, but by the grace of God, my husband managed to bring some sort of food home on a daily bases. It was seldom what we wanted, but it filled the stomach. On this one particular day, my baby and I were home alone, as we were five out of seven days of the week, when this commercial came on TV advertising some type of junk food. My baby, who was about two years old at that time, began to cry as he watched the food being plastered all over the screen saying, "Mommy, Mommy

I want." Knowing that we did not have anything of that sort in the house, and it had been weeks since we had, my heart began to sink as I took his hand and led him into the kitchen where I began to prepare a grilled cheese sandwich out of an end slice of bread and a small piece of "government cheese." That morsel of bread and cheese was all we had in the house, until my husband came home with our "manna" for that day. As I tried to hand the sandwich to him he pushed it away sobbing, "No Mommy no!" I took him in my arms and rocked him to sleep. As I sat there heartbroken for not being able to provide even something as simple as a cookie for my baby, I called out to God for divine intervention. I thought to myself, "Everyone is out there in the world being movers and shakers as they go about their lives." I felt so all alone—as if my baby and I were on a desert island with no one that could lend an ear to my cry. I said, "God *if* you hear me; let somebody bring me some money so I can buy a little "comfort food" for my babies."

The day went on and my other two children made it home, as well as my husband—who had with him our food for *that* day. We ate, and that night my husband went on to school. Around 8:00 p.m., the doorbell rang. I went to see who it was.

When I opened the door, my sister in the Lord, Colleen Keener, was standing there. She began passionately apologizing right off the bat. "I am so sorry!" she exclaimed, "I did not do what God told me to do. I got all the way home, and was in the process of taking off my clothes when He reminded me of His earlier instructions to go by your house, give you twenty dollars and take you to the store. Here I am, here it is, so let's go." I went to the store that night and did not buy beans, bread, rice or anything of that variety, but what I bought were: cookies, ice cream, chips, candy, and junk food for my babies. God actually heard me!

At that point, I held unimpeachable evidence that God hears me when I pray. I was no longer dubious, holding questioning faith, but my skepticism had now become my conviction. From that moment on, no one could ever tell me that God does not hear me when I pray. If there is anyone who has grown in their faith to the point of *knowing without a doubt* that God hears them every time they pray, then there has to be a landmark event that they can look back on, which would rejuvenate their faith in the event it ever began to get weak.

If you could see how much better off we are now than we were then—both naturally and more

so spiritually—you would know you must:
Pray There Before You Get There!

Everything Will Inevitably Work Out

There is no one on this earth who exists without experiencing problems, and by some "law of nature"—it is true—most troubles tend to work out in one way or another; maybe not the best way, but they work out someway or another. The destiny-defining question is, "Do you want to rely on things working themselves out in some unspecified or unknown way, or do you want to be certain that the perfect will of God for your life will come to fruition?" If the latter is your desire, then you must "pray" to assure yourself of that preferred result.

A majority of people think because they find some solace in a situation, that they have gotten an answer to their prayers, when in actuality, they have not. One has received a *true* answer to prayer when a divine intervention by the God of this universe is witnessed that leaves them proclaiming; "*Only God,* could have brought this thing to pass!"

Miracles didn't only happen in the Bible days, but they still occur in our day. They are not as rare as some are led to believe. I am sure a number of you (my precious readers) can say that you have personally experienced a miracle, or know someone who has. God performs miracles for the purpose of building faith.

Here is one of the many miracles God performed which brought awe to us during that blessed time we were experiencing. This is not by far the greatest miracle we received during that season, but is the one I feel noteworthy for this work:

Still during our time of trial and testing, one morning as I rose up out of my sleep to begin another day; God spoke these words to me, "Now I am going to move you into a realm of miracles." My spirit began to rejoice as I thought getting a brief moment of relief from our trials was at hand, but before that thought could reach its end, God began to speak again. "Be mindful of the fact that in order for a miracle to occur, the situation has to warrant a miracle," He admonished me, "So when adverse circumstances confront you, know that at that point, you are primed for a miracle."

During that time, God began to work miracle after miracle for me and my family. I will share this brief "one" for my ladies out there. I had gotten a bladder infection and was in anguish—you hear me ladies. I had just enough money to get the medication, if my doctor would call in a prescription for me. That was something he had done on a few occasions in past years, but this time when I called the office to have him call in a prescription he refused to do so unless I first came in for an exam. What an inopportune time for him to break from the norm. I only had enough money to pay for the medicine; not an exam and the medicine.

Being in much anguish, I was in need of a miracle! So I began to entreat God about what to do. God began to speak and He instructed me to go to my neighborhood apothecary. This pharmacy was not a part of a large store chain, but was a small little family-owned business. I had never patronized that establishment before, so why God would tell me to go there was a mystery to me. Knowing the voice of God—I immediately obeyed.

When I got there, I asked the owner if they had any over-the-counter medicine for a bladder infection. He directed me over to the shelf that held that kind of medication. I picked up a brand, paid for it and proceeded home, knowing all the time that the particular strength of medicine I purchased would not work, because I had tried it on prior occasions, all to no avail.

I arrived home and before I opened the package, I was impressed by the spirit to look at the expiration date. That was not something I would normally do, I just held trust that if the product was on the shelf, it was in the allotted time and safe to use. When I looked at the date it was so far out of date, that I could not believe it. Immediately, I picked up the phone and called the pharmacist and told him what had happened. He apologized and asked if I would bring it back in. In dire need of some relief, I complied.

When I arrived, he began to apologize again as he let me know that everything on his shelf was out of date and he did not know how that could have happened. I do not hold the belief that this was the norm for this pharmacy, but on this rare occasion, I believe it was a divine intervention by God. The pharmacist asked if I was allergic to sulfur, and upon my reply of "no," he offered to give me a prescription medication, at no extra cost. It was the same one I would have gotten if my doctor would have called it in for me.

I left there knowing that my God was a miracle worker. He could have instructed me to go to one of the larger chain pharmacies where I usually shopped, but He directed me to this little mom and pop shop, which up until that time, I had only driven by and perhaps taken a glance at. Only **God,** and **Him** only, could have brought this thing to pass! This did not just work out somehow, but it had to be a divine intervention from the God of the universe. He still works miracles!

I'll Make Prayer My Last Resort

Unwise individuals try to handle problems on their own. They first attempt everything known to man, and when they realize they can't produce, as a last resort, they seek the hand of God. By the time they make it to Him, their faith is weak or barely existent.

It is a depressing thought to try and comprehend the fact, that what too many Christians think is, "Well, I guess since I have exhausted everything else, I *should* pray." How sad! What they deem as prayer at that point is mere words they speak, to keep themselves from feeling guilty. They manage to mutter out a few words to God, which gives them some air of accomplishment and satisfaction, causing them to believe they have then met their obligation to Him. "Now, I have done what I am supposed to do," they spout—as if they were doing God a favor; not believing that what they prayed for would ever come to pass. If someone believed prayer was the tool to get them in touch with the all-knowing God, who possesses all the power needed to get them a desired result, they would have made it their first choice instead of their last resort. In order for one to ever experience the *joy* of answered prayer, this pattern of thinking has to be eradicated.

As we slowly bring the curtain down on the "Skeptic's Theory" we will say, "Yes, God does actually answer you when you pray, and all of the excuses you could ever dream up for not praying have been laid to rest." We have made it clear that there is always time for prayer, and one must learn to pray for themselves, because at the end of the day, you and you alone are responsible for your own prayer life. We have also showed how one can get the things they desire by not waiting to see if things are going to work out one way or another first, and then as a last resort, pray.

Once an individual learns how to pray, and stands assured of the fact that God hears them when they pray, they can, at that time, move from a prayer of fear on into different levels of faith in God.

> *"Prayer should always be an opening move, instead of a desperate remedy."*
> —Mary Simpson—

Chapter

4

Pray of Faith—Prayer of Fear

Exercising by doing water aerobics is one of my favorite hobbies, so I attend classes regularly on a continual basis. I was in the locker room after finishing up with an early morning class when one other female patron began to complain by saying, "I wish I could stop hurting!" Immediately my prayer radar went up, so I inquired of her as to where she was hurting. She responded directly by telling me she was hurting in her hip and down into her groin area. Knowing a lot about back pain, I told her that I was quite sure it was coming from her back because almost all leg pain has its origin in the back. Then I asked her if I could pray for her. With what I perceived as doubt she said, "Oh, OK, but I have prayed for myself and others have prayed for me—all to no avail." With confidence I said, "Nevertheless, I will pray, and I will **believe** God for you!" A lot of people call out words, but life-changing prayer is having faith in God and believing that what you ask for, He will grant.

I do not want to leave you with the impression that I am so naive as to believe that every person will be healed; even though that is one of the benefits Christians inherited as a result of Jesus' sacrifice when He suffered and died upon the cross. Experience has indeed made us aware of that fact. The apostle Paul (writer of 13 books of the New Testament Scriptures) had a thorn in his flesh of which he prayed earnestly thrice to have removed. God did not give Him what he asked for, but said to him, "My grace is sufficient for thee." I also know that theologians differ to what the thorn in Paul's flesh was. What we do know is it was an annoyance that kept him humble because of the great revelations he was receiving from God (2 Cor. 12:9). Elisha, who was one of God's Major Prophets, died of a sickness (2 Kings 13:14). He held a double portion of the anointing his predecessor Elijah had, but that still did not stop him from leaving this earth due to a sickness.

On another occasion, when I was in prayer

with a dear sister in the Lord over something that was weighing heavy on both of our hearts, God asked me this question, "What is the difference between a prayer of *Faith* and a prayer of *Fear*?" The question He had just proposed to me was a foundation for meditation to begin concerning the dissimilarities of the two opposing forces. Upon deep thought, thorough contemplation, and an in-depth investigation, I came up with these linguistic explanations regarding my beliefs: "A prayer of *Fear* is a prayer of disbelief in God's Word and in His abilities or willingness to perform what one is asking of Him. In that case, a prayer is probably being prayed something like this, "Lord I don't know, but if it's Thy will?" or "Lord, this disease will probably come upon me. You know my mom's third cousin on her uncle's father's side had this same thing." Fear cancels out faith. What you fear the most, will more than likely come upon you. We can call Job to give testimony to this truth, being that everything he feared came upon him. When Franklin D. Roosevelt said, "We have nothing to fear, but fear itself" he was also articulating a great truth, which has since haloed in the hearts of humans for centuries.

A prayer of fear is a prayer of agreement with Satan. A prayer of *Faith* is a prayer of belief in

God's Word—period! You come into agreement with God, and no matter what the portrayal of the circumstances which surround you are, you still *believe God.*

It is not the will of God, but there are some who pray out of desperation and panic—along with fear. They do not have sincere faith and belief in God's Word, or in His faithfulness and willingness to perform it. When Christians find themselves in an emotional or psychological upheaval, God is so awesome in that He will calm the tumult of His people. As God spoke to the waters of the sea and they become calm, so He speaks to the troubled hearts of His people to bring calm to their dilemmas also.

"You who still the noise of the seas, The noise of their waves, and the tumult of the [people]." (NKJV)

Ps. 65:7

After God calms the noisy sounds of chitter-chatter pursuant to fear in His children's lives, He assures them that they have managed to make the cut, and they are now a member of "Team Prayer." Since making the team, they have had some victories, and lost some games, all as a part of learning how to fight and win the ultimate battle. They are now poised to move on to greater challenges standing strong in faith, and holding a word in their mouth. Situations become subject to their commands, as they speak in faith and no longer in fear.

SAY

Part II

Graduate to the Next Level
Speak to your Situations and SAY

Say unto this Mountain be thou removed

And do not doubt in your heart

You shall have whatsoever you say

Chapter

5

Jesus—Elijah—Moses—Joshua

It is the unacquainted belief of some people that in order to get God to answer their prayers, they have to be someone "special," or hold a unique place with Him. God is no respecter of person, but He is a respecter of faith and spirit. There are those who have developed their faith to a level where they can—without hindrance—enter the presence of God and speak with Him one on one, then at their word, He begins to move. They are not born into Christendom this way, but from faith to faith, they rise to this level of spiritual prominence.

Christians first go through the infant stage of being babes in Christ, where God gives them whatever they ask for, in order to build their faith and trust in Him. However, in apprehension that He might raise a bunch of spoiled brats, God slowly, lovingly, and carefully moves His protégées to the next phase, wherein they do not receive everything they ask for. After they master that phase with flying colors, they then mature to level three. By this time, they have learned so much about God and how He operates, until not receiving exactly what they ask for would not faze them. To that they declare with confidence, "If you don't God—I know that you can."

Lastly, God's protégées progress to the final phase of preparation, and as they graduate, they toss their caps into the sky while declaring with all that is within them, "You **can't tell me** that there is anything my God is not able to do!" At that point, because of the level of faith they have come to enjoy, they are afforded the power and anointing to move the hand of God; and along with that, they are moreover poised to be able to take dominion over atmospheric conditions, as the elements of wind, cold, rain, sunshine, and the rest, become subject to their words.

Let's give case in point:
Matthew Henry sums this up for us in just a few words, like only he could.

The Commentator quoted:

"How easily this was done, with a word's speaking. Moses commanded the waters with a rod; Joshua, with the Ark of the Covenant; Elisha, with the prophet's mantle; but Christ with a word. See His absolute dominion over all the creatures, which (speaks of) both His honor, and the happiness of those that have Him on their side."

Elijah Prayed and It Did Not Rain

Elijah was a giant in the spirit, standing tall as one of God's Major Prophets. He prayed that the heavens would not give neither dew nor rain, but at his word—and the heavens shut up for three and one-half years. He was a man, no different than you and I, and as he prayed, God heard his petition and moved according to his words.

"And Elijah the Tishbite, who was of the inhabitants of Gilead, said unto Ahab, As the LORD God of Israel liveth, before whom I stand, there shall not be dew nor rain these years, but according to my word."

1 Kings 17:1

"Elias [Elijah] was a man subject to like passions as we are, and he prayed earnestly that it might not rain: and it rained not on the earth by the space of three years and six months. And he prayed again, and the heaven gave rain, and the earth brought forth her fruit."

James 5:17-18

In this, we have account one.

Moses Commanded the Waters

After the children of Israel left behind the torture of their enslaved lives in Egypt, they began their journey through the great and terrible wilderness, *en route* to the land flowing with milk and honey God had promised them.

While journeying, they soon came upon the Red Sea and found they had nowhere to go. With the waters of the Red Sea in front of them, and Pharaoh and his army in hot pursuit behind them, they needed a miracle.

Moses used the rod given to him by God and he stretched it over the Sea. The waters parted and the children of Israel walked through on dry land. God had the power, but Moses had the authority to command the waters.

In this, we have account two.

Jesus Spoke to the Wind and Waters

*J*esus was the son of God, but while here on earth, He walked as a man. He had the authority to speak to the elements of wind and water, and at His command they obeyed Him.

"Now it came to pass on a certain day, that He went into a ship with His disciples: and He said unto them, Let us go over unto the other side of the lake. And they launched forth. But as they sailed He fell asleep: and there came down a storm of wind on the lake; and they were filled with water, and were in jeopardy. And they came to Him, and awoke Him, saying, Master, Master, we perish. Then He arose, and rebuked the wind and the raging of the water: and they ceased, and there was a calm. And He said unto them, Where is your faith? And they being afraid wondered, saying one to another, What manner of man is this! for He [commands] even the winds and water, and they obey Him."

Luke 8:22-25

Jesus is our example, and if He has the authority to speak to the wind and waters and they obey Him, then why not us? We are the children of God also, and walk in the same power, which grants us authority to speak to situations and conditions in our life, and have them move at our word.

In this, we have account three.

The Sun Stood Still and the Moon Stayed

The children of Israel were in a fierce battle with their arch enemies, the Amorites. This day in history will forever be spoken of because its account lies in the ever-unfolding pages of Scripture. On this particular day, God performed a miracle so stupendously grand, until it has never been witnessed again.

That noted day probably started out as any other day. The sun came up over the horizon at the same time, and positioned itself in the same place it had from the moment God first hung it in the sky. Who knew, that before this day would end, it would somehow be united with the following day, converting the two days into the longest day in history.

Early this historic day, the sun made its way over the carrot-colored horizon, bringing with it light that the Israelites needed for their battle. By the middle of the day, the sun shone its brightest, as they were in the heat of battle. Finally, the sun began its downward swing, and darkness was ultimately going to enter the battle, becoming an enemy to the children of God and a friend to the Amorites.

With daylight losing its luster, and the sun soon to hide its face behind the hills of Ajalon, the Israelites were losing their advantage; so Joshua, who was Israel's leader, prayed to God for help. After his prayer, Joshua subsequently got so inspired until he spoke to the sun and moon and commanded them to still their position in the sky. God, being a god that fights for His people, harkened to Joshua's prayers. He altered the course of nature so that the two major heavenly bodies stood still for 24 hours, prolonging the day until the Israelites could finish the battle, and achieve the victory.

"Then spake Joshua to the LORD in the day when the LORD delivered up the Amorites before the children of Israel, and he said in the sight of Israel, 'Sun, stand thou still upon Gibeon; and thou, Moon,

in the valley of Ajalon. And the sun stood still, and the moon stayed, until the people had avenged themselves upon their enemies. Is not this written in the book of Jasher? So the sun stood still in the midst of heaven, and hasted not to go down about a whole day. And there was no day like that before it or after it, that the LORD hearkened unto the voice of a man for the LORD fought for Israel."

Joshua 10:12-14

There was never a day like that before and has never been a day since where God so harkened to the request of a man, and a people as they through faith and prayer, petitioned Him.

In this, we have account four.

Is there anything too hard for the Lord?

In these four accounts, we observe miracles being performed by a word spoken from the mouth of humans who were no different than you and I. In my heart of hearts, I am persuaded that similar things can happen if we, through faith and obedience, realize who we are in God, and understand the power and authority that lies within our mouth.

Chapter 6

Believing Prayer Pulls Down Divine Aid

I was *en route* back home to Denver, Colorado, from a recent trip to Houston, Texas, and as I sat cozily in the first-class cabin of an Airbus 320 looking out over the rose-colored sky, full of billowing clouds that seemed to float by with ease, the captain's voice came over the intercom. He seemed a bit frazzled as he made the announcement that we were about 80 miles out from Denver and about five minutes away from some inclement weather, producing heavy thunderstorms that would imminently cause the aircraft to take some sharp jolts. With these words already out of his mouth, he immediately tried to bring comfort by informing us that we and the aircraft were not in any danger. If you fly with any degree of frequency, this is probably something similar to any given announcement you have heard from time to time, especially flying over the Rockies during thunderstorm season. I have heard this message at varied times in my many travels, but this time there was something a bit different in the captain's voice. He went on to say that he was going to turn the 'Fasten seat belt' sign on in a couple of minutes, and if we had a need to move about the aircraft, or use the lavatory, we should get it done quickly. He also said that we would not be able to get up or move about again until we landed, because the thunderstorms were so severe. In his announcement, he went on to tell the flight attendants to finish servicing the cabin quickly, and then take their jump seats.

When I heard those somewhat alarming words from the captain, God began to speak to me these simple, but profound situation-altering words, **"Pray There Before You Get There."** With those words ringing down in my soul, God continued to speak. If what lies ahead has been revealed, and it is adverse to what you want, **Pray There Before You Get There**. Send the Word of God ahead for you to alter the conditions, and make the atmosphere conducive, before you get there. Dispatch angels to go in front to do the work that needs to be done ahead of time. Why wait until you are in the middle of a crisis to begin praying. When disaster is foretold and you have the knowledge, power, and authority to do something, then move on it.

I could not tell you what the dialogue between the captain and the air traffic controller was, because I did not deem it necessary to tune to channel nine and become privy to their conversation. My focus was on talking with the only one that could do something about our situation. I began to pray, "Lord, smooth out the airways so we won't have such a bumpy arrival into Denver. Clear a pathway for us to get through, in the name of Jesus." It was just that simple.

I continued to sit there, looking out of the window, while the skies grew darker and darker as we neared our destination. The closer we got, the more focused I became on what God had just spoken to my spirit. I thought to myself, "Well, no bumps or jolts yet, and I know we have been flying longer than five, or even ten minutes." Soon after those thoughts passed through my head the captain returned to the intercom and said with somewhat of an implausible sigh of relief, "Well we made it through that, but I am going to leave the 'Fasten seat belt' light on until we land in Denver; because you never know what could happen." We drew closer and closer and nothing happened, even closer and closer and still nothing happened. We finally landed on the tarmac with a *beautiful* landing. I looked over at my husband, who was sitting beside me, and asked him if he felt any bumps or jolts. He said, "No, I did not feel anything." At that point, I made him privy to the conversation God and I just had. With amazement he said, "I am sure glad to be married to a *'Woman of God'*."

With everything said and done, we were finally at the gate, and the captain once again came across the intercom and said, "Well the First Officer navigated us through that one." I leaned over to my husband and said, "The First Officer was in the third seat; the captain of the plane was in the second seat, and my God (the Captain of Captains) was at the helm of this aircraft. Before those words could fall afresh on my husband's ears, the awe-stricken and thankful captain returned to the intercom once again. Displaying relief and reverence to a power much greater than he was, he proclaimed, "Somebody on this plane must be living right, because that was not suppose to have happened." His final words to us before we disembarked were, "Because the thunderstorms are so severe, ours is the last aircraft that was allowed to land. They have now closed the airport, and no other aircraft can take off or land at this time. Have a nice evening." My God's final words to me were: ***"Pray There Before You Get There."***

After over 20 years of flying all over the world, through all types of situations and weather conditions; this time my husband and I left the aircraft, walked down the "Jetway," and on through the concourse with a new found revelation on how good God is. This revelation took root in our hearts, and we were not about to let this eye opener soon be forgotten.

What can't He do, who has done this?

Upon my arrival home, God began to open up an even greater revelation concerning what we had just experienced. He began to reveal to me what that same situation we had experienced in the natural, looked like in the spiritual realm. He reminded me that things we encounter in life are first natural, then they are spiritual (1 Cor. 15:46). When Jesus spoke, He did so mostly in parables saying, "The kingdom of Heaven is like…" All of the afore-mentioned testimony happened in the natural, but let us take a deeper, spiritual look at the same situation.

Spiritually, as one is *en route* toward a targeted destination, they can find themselves in the middle of a turbulent storm, too far in to turn around; and not yet at their point of destination. As they stand and look back, they are caught betwixt and between; having no desire to turn around, because what they just went through was too terrible to ever want to turn back into, and that which is positioned ahead does not motivate them to be inclined to plunge onward—head first.

There also are times when one is not afforded the opportunity to stand still in a holding pattern, because in that situation they might become a sitting target for an armed attack.

So the destiny-defining question is, "What do I do now?" Answer: "You pray and seek God for His will." If He says move forward, then you move forward, pressing on toward your purpose, believing that God will see you through. If He says stand still, then you stand still believing that you are resting under the shadows of the Almighty, and nothing shall by any means harm you. If He says turn around and go back, then you turn around and go back; because on rare occasions we may have to go back and retrace our steps as we cover the same ground again, seeing that we did not get the message God wanted us to get the first time through.

Pray There Before You Get There!

KEY

Part III

Wisdom and Knowledge is the KEY
Information Only Understood by Specialists

Know how to always get answers to your prayers

Entrust God with the responsibility of answered prayer

Yield your will to God's will

Chapter 7

How to Always Get Answers to Your Prayers

Eleven dynamic principles of effective prayer:

Is it possible for any Christian to get answers to what they perceive as difficult, or even a simple request made unto God? Yes it is possible, if they know how to ask.

Here is a list of things Christians should adhere to as they begin to seek God for answers to their heartfelt prayers:

Come Boldly Before the Throne of God

"Let us therefore come boldly unto the throne of grace that we may obtain mercy, and find grace to help in time of need."

Heb. 4:16

There is a certain air about a person who knows who they are. They don't display arrogance, but they exude confidence. So we should *never* walk up to the throne of God nonchalantly; or as a wayward child. This is totally opposite of the way God desires that we come before Him. We should come before God's throne as the prince, or princess, whose father is the King of Kings. It is imperative that we know who we are in God, and who He is to us.

When we have confidence, we can come boldly before our Father; knowing already without any doubt, that before we ask, we are going to get what we desire. No first-rate father would ever withhold any good thing from his child, if they walk upright before him. Just think of the wealthiest daughter in the world, the well-known, Vanisha Mittal, heiress of 51 billion dollars, and *if* you can, now allow your thoughts to progress past that vision; see yourself standing before your "Father God," and realize that you are wealthier than that. With that thought anchored in heart, *now,* come boldly before the throne of God.

Ask the Father in the Name of Jesus

When we make our petitions, we do not ask Jesus for what we want, but we ask God, our Father, in the name of Jesus, His Son. Through the name of Jesus, and only through that name, are we able to directly approach the throne of God in prayer. God has highly exalted His son and given Him a name that is above every name that *"At the name of Jesus every knee must bow and every tongue confess that Jesus is Lord."* The father has bestowed this honor upon His Son, because of the ultimate sacrifice He made when He died upon the cross and became a ransom for our sins. Jesus, who knew no sin, became sin for us, so when the Father looks at us He sees no sin, because our sins are covered under the blood of Jesus' sacrifice.

"And in that day ye shall ask Me nothing. Verily, verily, I say unto you, [whatsoever] ye shall ask the Father in My Name, He will give it you."

John 16:23

Power has been given to the name of Jesus to heal the sick, cast out demons, and bring deliverance; and there is no other name under the heavens, whereby humans might get saved. When applied, the name of Jesus was known to hold so much power, until His disciples were commanded not to speak or teach anymore in that name. The name of Jesus is a strong tower, and Christians can run into it and find strength and safety.

Ask in Faith Nothing Wavering
Our Faith Must Stand Sure

Confident prayer is having faith, without wavering. If we waver, we should not think that we will get anything from God.

How do we waver?

- One day up, the next day down.
- One day God can do anything! The next day, except this.
- One day up on a mountaintop, the next day, down in a valley.
- One day excited about life, the next day, down in the dumps.

We must stay constant, steady, and unvarying in our trust in God, and in His ability to bring to pass the things we believe Him for. Without faith, it is impossible to please God. Those who come to Him must believe that He is and that He will reward them that seek Him (Heb. 11:6). That being said, we can piggyback on the term "come boldly," by saying, "We waver when we do not know who we are." Or maybe we do know who we are, and realize that because of the state of sin we are in; we cannot come boldly before God's throne. When we know who we are, then and only then can we come boldly before the throne of God (our Father) and ask Him for what we desire without wavering in doubt and unbelief.

"But let him ask in faith, nothing wavering. For he that wavereth is like a wave of the sea driven with the wind and tossed. For let not that man think that he shall receive [anything] of the Lord."

James 1:6-7

Pray the Word of God

If someone is in search for bricks to begin construction on a prayer fortress, they should look no further than the promises of God, which is the best material to use in laying a foundation of prayer.

Providing one desires to use the Word of God effectively, they must first become proficient in it. They must become familiar enough with Scripture to be able to use it in any given situation. God does not move otherwise, but on His Word, and He watches over His Word to perform it. If He said it, He will do it, and if He spoke it, He is faithful to bring it to pass.

The practice of getting into the Word of God on a constant basis is what we must adhere to, because faith comes by "hearing and hearing," "again and again," the Word of God "over and over," until it becomes so much a part of you, that it can be spoken impromptu from your spirit. When Satan came to tempt Jesus after His forty-day fast, Jesus was able to quote the Word of God pursuant to every enticing suggestion Satan brought up.

God desires that we know His Word, and prove our case with it. He said in Isaiah 43:26, that we should put Him in remembrance of His Word, so that by using it to reason with Him, we might be justified.

Pray God's Will

God's will is found in His Word, and He honors His Word even above His name. In order to pray, and be assured that you will get a positive response to your prayers, you must pray God's will. If you have yet to get to the point where you are able to hear and understand the voice of God when He speaks to your spirit, then all you have as a resource is the Written Word; which is not altogether a bad thing, because God will not speak to your spirit anything that is outside of His Word anyway. I have often said that there isn't anything we can face in this life without an example being laid out in the Word of God, which gives us an answer to our dilemma.

"And this is the confidence that we have in Him, that, if we ask [anything] according to His will, He heareth us: and if we know that He [hears] us, whatsoever we ask, we know that we have the petitions that we desired of Him."

1 John 5:14-15

Realizing that there are so many different variables in any given situation, we cannot just give blanket answers to questions asked by the people of God. We must be practical in our responses to their queries. I have had this sort of statement and question proposed to me on numerous occasions, "I know God's will is found in His Word, and He answers prayers accordingly," but what about a question like, "God, should I take this job or that one? I can't find an answer to that in God's Word, can I?" That's a tough question, but there is an answer. God has dreams, desires, and visions for each of our lives individually. We must spend enough time in the presence of God while reading and meditating upon His Word to the extent we develop a relationship with Him, and we are mature enough to discern His voice. God will speak the "counsel" of His will to us (Eph. 1:11). He will not just let us know His will, but He will advise us on how we must carry out His will. God speaks to our inner being (our spirit), by The Holy Ghost. He will lead and direct us into all truth.

My personal experiences to answer this query are:

Let's first go to Scripture: When King David asked God if he should pursue the Amalekites who had came into Ziklag, burned it with fire, and took their women and children; God spoke to him, and instructed him to pursue and recover all.

There was a time I asked God a question on whether I should continue to pursue after this particular thing I was seeking, and had been turned down for three times before, or should I just quit, and accept the answer "No." I was once given awesome advice by someone who said to me, "Never accept a 'No' from someone who does not have the power to give you a 'Yes'." (That was for free.) But God, in His infinite wisdom, answered me by taking me to the same scripture referenced above. When I read the part, "pursue and recover all," my spirit connected to that Word, and I knew with surety God had given me my answer. I pursued and recovered all I expected, and even more.

On one other occasion, I was being encouraged by my superiors, as well as subordinates, to apply for this new position that had just opened up on my job. I was not sure if that scenario was the will of God for my life, or not. I did not know if I would be making a drastic mistake in choosing to move up to a different position, at that particular time in my career.

I was on this fast track, and had moved up so quickly in the company, until everyone believed in me and was awe-struck. But I was intelligent enough to know that the other position entailed a lot of duties in which I was not proficient. Nevertheless, I thought, "Well they believe in me, maybe I can."

Dubious, I went to God for an answer. He once again led me to a Scripture in His Word, which up until that time, I had no knowledge of. Romans 12:16 instructed me to, "Mind not high things." The 1599 Geneva Bible notes state: There is nothing that disrupts harmony like seeking glory. I was being pumped up by everyone around me—because of my already accelerated track of promotions—to seek for something that was too high for me.

Seeking vainglory from them would have cost me my already secure job. Realizing I probably would have gotten the new position if I would have applied for it, I did not take the chance, but I remained at my place of duty, and achieved enormous success with that company, in my then present role of responsibility.

I shared these two episodes of my life to testify to the fact that the answers I was seeking, were still found in the Word of God, but indirectly. God can speak to us in a myriad of ways. Because He is a spirit and we are spirit beings—who have a soul and live in a body—He speaks to us Spirit to spirit; however, when He chooses to speak to our spirit, it's never in contradiction to what's in His

Word.

"And thine ears shall hear a word behind thee, saying, This is the way, walk ye in it, when ye turn to the right hand, and when ye turn to the left."

Isa. 30:21

God is God, and in His omniscience, He knows the beginning and the end. He also knows His will for our life, and the path we should follow. As a natural Shepard sees after His sheep, so God walks behind us, and if we get off track, we will hear His voice behind us—in our spiritual ears—telling us which way we should go.

In addition to the above stated form of communication, God speaks His will through His Word, as well as other people, things, and situations, to such a degree it can be said His methods are infinite. We must not put God in a box to say that He only does a certain thing a certain way, every time, but we must allow Him to be GOD. He will speak His will to whomever; whenever, however, and wherever He chooses. God finds a way in which each individual can personally understand Him, and then He speaks.

Pray Fervently

One should not be as flippant as to half-heartedly rattle off a few memorized prayers to God at bedtime, but they should pray with their whole heart. They should approach the throne of God with passion, purpose and a predetermined will not to let Him go, until He blesses them.

"...The effectual fervent prayer of a righteous man [avails] much."

James 5:16

When I examined this scripture, I observed three words that caught my attention:

1. Effectual

2. Fervent

3. Righteous

If one is to get answers to their prayers, all three entities must work together, as in a relay. Effectual starts the race, because if someone does not have the mind to be potentially successful, then there is no need to begin their prayer pursuit. Effectual hands off to fervent, fervency kicks in with passion and enthusiasm, bringing intensity and fire to the second leg of the race. Fervent hands off to righteous and righteousness justifies, and stands blameless as it avails in crossing the finish-line, and receives the blue-ribbon of answered prayers.

Answers to our prayers are not given because of the sheer number of words we use, or the way they are articulated, but answers to prayers lie in the sincerity and fervency with which they are requested.

The most fervent prayer we can find in scripture is when Jesus prayed until sweat fell from Him like drops of blood (Luke 22:44). In His state of humanness, He did not want to face death on the cross and be separated from His Father. Jesus, being the Son of God, prayed fervently in His most distressing hour. Even though Jesus prayed with much fervency, God could not grant His request, because our destiny lied on the other side of His obedience.

Hannah's husband loved her, but that did not suffice; she had a deep need for more. She desired a child from the Lord, thus she prayed for a child until she was sore. She prayed so emotionally until the priest who was in the temple, thought she was drunk at that early morning hour (1 Sam. 1:10).

> *"We rail, we yell, we wail,*
> *then turn pale as we exhale,*
> *but when all else fails,*
> *sheer Fervency in prayer avails."*
> —*Mary Simpson*—

Be Persistent

As Christians, it is a must that we possess purposeful determination, refusing to give up or let go, as we endeavor to get answers to our most needy situations. Possessing tenacity, we must be relentless as we ask, and keep on asking, seek, and keep on seeking, knock, and keep on knocking, waiting for the doors to be opened unto us. Holding fast to our position and purpose, we must keep on enduring pass the point when the "average Christian" would have the propensity to give up.

"Then He spoke a parable to them, that men always ought to pray and not lose heart, saying: "There was in a certain city a judge who did not fear God nor regard man. Now there was a widow in that city; and she came to him, saying, 'Get justice for me from my adversary.' And he would not for a while; but afterward he said within himself, 'Though I do

not fear God nor regard man, yet because this widow troubles me I will avenge her, lest by her continual coming she weary me.'" Then the Lord said, "Hear what the unjust judge said. And shall God not avenge His own elect who cry out day and night to Him, though He bears long with them? I tell you that He will avenge them speedily." (NKJV)

Luke 18:1-8

The widow, in her "wearisome persistence," was unrelenting in her endeavor to get what she wanted. We should be like-minded as we pursue after the things we desire from God.

Another case of persistence:

The "woman of Canaan" came to Jesus and cried out, *"Have mercy on me, O Lord, thou Son of David; my daughter is grievously vexed with a devil."* He did not answer her, but she came again and she worshipped him this time, saying, *"Lord, help me."* At that point, Jesus treated her as if she did not deserve what she was requesting of Him, but that did not deter her. She came back with a rhetorical reply, and Jesus being just, held no other resort, but to answer her. Jesus' response to her was, *"O woman, great is thy faith: be it unto thee even as thou wilt."* And her daughter was made whole from that very hour (Matt. 15:22-28).

In these two examples of persistence, we can conclude that if we continually come to the throne of God, determined not to stop until He blesses us, we will get the things we desire of Him.

God moves according to our faith, and our faith is shown in our persistence and steadfastness.

Worship Him, and Give Praise and Thanks

When wanting to receive answers to prayer, we must give praise and thanks in advance, during, and after the fact; for this is the will of God concerning us.

"Be careful for nothing; but in [everything] by prayer and supplication with thanksgiving let your requests be made known unto God."

Phil. 4:6

Silas and the Apostle Paul were locked up in prison, and Scripture professes that at midnight, they began to sing praises unto God. Then suddenly there was a great earthquake. At that point, the foundation of the prison was shaken, the doors sprang open, and they were loosed from their bonds (Acts 16:25-26). When the praises go up, the blessings come down.

This thought segues into another one of my many testimonies. One day a few years back, as I was sitting at my desk at home, I held no thought of getting anything from God. I just wanted to praise Him. I began to sing praises unto God for an hour and a half, singing these very words continually, "When the praises go up, the blessings come down, when the praises go up, the blessings come down, when the praises go up, the blessings come down, (you can sing along with me, come on if you know it) when the praises go up, the blessings come down, when the praises go up, the blessings come down." At the end of my one and a half hour singing spree, where I was singing these words over, and over, and over, and over, God spoke these words to me, "Now reach up, and pull down that which you desire."

Astounded as I heard Him say that, I found my mind focusing on this white Lexus I had desired for a while. As I continued with my singing, I began to reach up, as if I was actually pulling down the car I was visualizing. After having touched the heart of God and not being a selfish wife, I began to pull down a red Jeep Grand

Cherokee for my wonderful husband, Will. Ah!

That very month, God gave me the money I needed, and I walked into the Stevenson Creek Lexus dealership in San Jose, California, and paid cash for my brand new Lexus. The same day my husband drove home his shiny new red Jeep. When we worship God, and do so in spirit and truth, we touch His heart, and at that point, the windows of heaven are opened to us.

> *"Once you move God's heart*
> *you can then move His hand."*
> —Mary Simpson—

Forgive Others

We must find room in our hearts to forgive others, and not forget that God forgave us for our many sins. Where would we be had He not forgiven us? We cannot allow our mind to go that far left for fear that the vision might leave an indelible imprint we do not want to hold on to.

"Therefore if thou bring thy gift to the altar, and there [remember] that thy brother hath ought against thee; leave there thy gift before the altar, and go thy way; first be reconciled to thy brother, and then

come and offer thy gift."

Matt. 5:23-24

"For if ye forgive men their trespasses, your heavenly Father will also forgive you: But if ye forgive not men their trespasses, neither will your Father forgive your [trespasses]."

Matt. 6:14-15

Forgiveness breeds forgiveness; therefore, if we desire forgiveness, we must forgive.

It is my firm belief that the ultimate act of forgiveness is to be able to ask God to forgive someone, as you lay dying. With life draining out of your limp body, you look at their blood-soaked hands, realizing that it is your blood you see, and you can still say, "Father forgive them."

"And they stoned Stephen, calling upon God, and saying, Lord Jesus, receive my spirit. And he kneeled down, and cried with a loud voice, Lord, lay not this sin to their charge. And when he had said this, he fell asleep."

Acts 7:59-60

As Jesus was hanging upon the cross with His blood upon his executioner's hands, He prayed, *"Father forgive them for they know not what they do"* (Luke 23:34).

> "Forgiveness releases the one who has been wronged—to be right."
>
> —*Mary Simpson*—

Apply Spiritual Authority

On certain occasions, God desires that as Holy Ghost-filled believers, we take charge, and use the spiritual authority we have been granted, to handle our own problems.

"And the LORD said unto Moses, Wherefore [cry] thou unto me? [Speak] unto the children of Israel, that they go forward."

Ex. 14:15

Speak to a situation:

God has given to us as believers, the authority to speak to situations and have them turn around in our favor.

"For verily I say unto you, That whosoever shall <u>say unto this mountain</u>, Be thou removed, and be thou cast into the sea; and shall not doubt in his heart, but shall believe that those things which he saith shall come to pass; he shall have whatsoever he saith."

Mark 11:23

It is imperative that we as Christians begin to speak to situations that confront us, and watch them change.

- Speak to sickness and declare the Word of God that says, *"With His stripes we are healed,"* (Isa. 53:5). Not just healed in my body, but my whole being is healed.

- Speak to your wayward children, and declare, *"As [for] me and my house, we will serve the Lord,"* (Josh. 24:15).

- Speak to a bad marriage and affirm the sanctity of it in that the Word said, *"Whoso [finds] a wife [finds] a good thing, and [obtains] [favor] of the LORD* (Prov. 18:22).

- Speak to an empty bank account and declare the will of God which states in Job 36:11: *"If they obey and serve him, they shall spend their days in prosperity, and their years in pleasures."*

If we do not open our mouth and begin to *"say"*

to our situations, by speaking the Word of God over them, then God has nothing to move on. A closed mouth leaves doors closed.

Decree a thing:
> *"Thou [shall] also <u>decree a thing,</u> and it shall be established unto thee: and the light shall shine upon thy ways."*
>
> Job 22:28

The thing that God has already willed, will be established unto you, for *"Who is he who speaks and it comes to pass, when the Lord has not commanded it"* (Lam. 3:37; NKJV)? When we open our mouth to decree a thing it is the Lord that has already commanded it.

As someone spends enough time in the presence of God to know and understand His heart, they can speak a thing and God will establish it, because as that individual begins to decree a thing, they will be speaking the heart of God.

> *"For thou, O LORD of hosts, God of Israel, hast revealed to thy servant, saying, I will build thee an house: therefore hath thy servant found in his heart to pray this prayer unto Thee."*
>
> 2 Sam. 7:27

David knew what was in God's heart, so at that point, he prayed the heart of God back to God. The Lord spoke it, so David pursued after it.

When we decree a thing, the step by step guide of its travels is as follows:
That decreed thing starts in the heart of God. It travels from God's heart to God's mouth, then travels from God's mouth to our ears, then journeys from our ears, to our heart, from our heart it travels to our mouth, from our mouth it travels back to God's ears, then into existence.

Bind and loose:
We, as blood-washed believers, have been given authority by God to bind the hand of Satan, along with his demons, and *forbid* their work by overruling them, and driving them out of the body and soul of humans. We possess the authority to stop the onslaught of sickness, disease, and destruction of every sort, over our life, as well as the lives of others we care about. We have authority, through the name of Jesus, to speak to the powers of darkness and command that they cease.

> *And the seventy returned again with joy, saying, Lord, even the devils are subject unto us through Thy name.*
>
> Luke 10:17

Our job as authority possessors is to use that which has been given to us by God, to forbid Satan and stop him in his tracks. In order to see deliverances take place, we must *first* bind (forbid) the works of the strongman, who is Satan, and destroy his power, along with the influence he has over the lives and situations of individuals. Once the strongman has been forbidden, and his hands tied, he can no longer do the work of destruction he planned for us. Matt. 12:29 offers testimony to this: *"Or else how can one enter into a strong man's house, and spoil his goods, except he first bind the strong man? [And] then he will spoil his house."*

After the powers of darkness have been bound, we also possess the authority to loose the spirit of God, to go in and do the work that is needed at any given place and time. To loose is to allow a person or thing to go free.

Jesus used the power and authority that He possessed to loose the woman who had an infirmity for twelve long years.

And when Jesus saw her, He called her to Him, and said unto her, Woman, thou art loosed from thine infirmity.

Luke 13:12

Jesus spoke a word to her in authority, and she received her healing.

We can resist Satan and he will leave us for a season, and we can also destroy his works and influence over our life, but we can't bind him utterly, because he is the prince of the air, and he goes about seeking whom he may devour (Eph. 2:2). In the millennial reign, Satan will be completely bound in chains by the angels of God for 1,000 years, but will be loosed again after that (Rev. 20:1-3). Even though we have not been given the power to completely bind Satan, we have been authorized to forbid his works over our lives.

Prophesy:

In the sense we are going to use it, the term "prophesy" is foretelling the future; even though, we know that the term "prophesy" is also used in another sense. That sense being, possessing great revelation of the Scripture, and having the ability to get it across to others.

"*Having then gifts differing according to the*

> *grace that is given to us, whether prophecy, let us <u>prophesy</u> according to the proportion of faith..."*
>
> Rom. 12:6

Whenever we prophesy, it must be done pursuant to the will, purpose, and instruction of God, whether we are foretelling the future or revealing revelation from the Word of God. At the point, we receive revelation from the Word of God concerning our life, we are then able to apply it to our life. If we do not know what the Word of God says concerning His will for us, we cannot claim it for our future. Understanding the plan of God for your life will then afford you the insight to be able to call those future things and events into your life as if they already were. You can speak the Word of God over a situation and declare, "I am what the Word of God says that I am. I can do what the word of God says I can do. I call into existence the things that I desire for my life. I call in peace, prosperity, love, joy, rest, determination, direction, guidance, and instruction. I call forth children and grandchildren, along with their salvation. I call in health and healing, favor and promotion. I call it in, and so be it, in the matchless name of Jesus Christ my Lord! Amen.

This is not that "name it and claim it" phenomenon that went across the church world like a whirlwind, a few years back; but, this is having faith in the Word of God and proclaiming it over your life, knowing that God is faithful to His Word, and He stands behind it and backs it up.

Be Precise

God said that if an individual's ways pleased Him, then He would give to that person the desires of their heart (Ps. 37:4); not just anything, but what that person has targeted in their heart. Everyone has specific things they desire.

Being ambiguous is no way to get what you need from God. As we lay our petitions out before Him in faith, we should not just say, "Lord give me whatever," and when we get "whatever," we are upset with God. We must be right on target with our request. There is a much used saying that goes, "Aim for nothing and hit it every time." James 4:2 says we have not because we ask not, so we must ask, and ask for exactly what we want.

Being a marriage educator, as well as a Board Certified Pastoral Counselor, I have heard many wives make statements like, "My husband should know what I want. I'm not going to tell him." My wisdom to them is, "Maybe he does, and maybe he doesn't. Maybe he should; but if you want to get exactly what you desire, you had better let him know, "what you want"—"when you want it"—"how you want it"—and "where you want it," or you will be the one to lose out.

Being passive, and not dialoguing when you desire something *a whole lot,* is not a wise thing to do.

> *"You can ask once, twice, or, thrice,*
> *but being precise will get you*
> *your answer in a trice."*
> —Mary Simpson—

Chapter 8

Nine Reasons for Unanswered Prayer

Lack of Faith

Many times, faith starts out strong, but ends up weak or nonexistent. We start out in faith, but lose it somewhere along the way, before the answer gets there. The apostle Paul in Hebrews 10:35-37, tell us to, *"Cast not away therefore your confidence, which hath great [recompense] of reward. For ye have need of patience, that, after ye have done the will of God, ye might receive the promise. For yet a little while, and He that shall come will come, and will not tarry."* Because of warfare, your answers may be held up in the atmosphere. Daniel waited 21 days for an answer to his prayer (Dan 10:12). He did not realize his answer was sent as soon as he prayed; however, in faith he still waited. True faith has the ability to wait.

Wrong Reason Wrong Season

On some occasions, one may have to wait days, months, years, or even decades until the right time and season for some prayers to be answered. God may cause us to wait until the time is right for Him to be able to get the most *glory* out of the show of His power. We all know that whatever we do here on earth is all about Him (God) anyway. When more people are able to witness answered prayer, the faith of a greater number of people will be increased.

"And therefore will the LORD wait, that He may be gracious unto you, and therefore will He be exalted, that He may have mercy upon you: for the LORD is a God of judgment: blessed are all they that wait for Him."

Isa. 30:18

"For the vision is yet for an appointed time, but at

the end it shall speak, and not lie: though it tarry, wait for it; because it will surely come, it will not tarry."

Hab. 2:3

"To [everything] there is a season, and a time to every purpose under the heaven..."

Eccl. 3:1

We must wait for our season and not faint as we stand in faith and hope in our God, who will ultimately bring to pass what we believe Him for. Our hope in Him will not allow us to face shame.

Wavering

We waver when we do not take the Word of God at face value. What He said, we must simply believe. We should not start over-analyzing the Word of God, as we try to put a human spin on a divine thing. In so doing, we are setting our hearts up to begin to wonder and thereby waver. Our ditherer begins, "Maybe He can, or maybe He can't. Maybe He will, and then maybe He won't." James 1:8 states, *"A double minded man is unstable in all his ways."* Possessing unwavering faith is a necessity in our attempt to move the hand of God. Once we start wondering, we become unstable in our faith, and we are then as an object being tossed around by the wind.

Satan, at that point, will find an occasion to try and place more doubt in our minds, but we must thwart his plans instantly. When he tries to speak, we must use a peremptory strike and not let him get a word in edgewise.

Not Asking According to God's Will

The prophets of old would pray to God, and because there was no doubt, they received exactly what they were requesting. Elijah did not have any doubt that God would do it when he called on God to send down fire upon mount Carmel, and the sacrifice. I wonder why? Answer: "Elijah was so close to God and stayed in constant communion and fellowship with Him until he knew the will of God beforehand."

"And this is the confidence that we have in Him, that, if we ask [anything] according to His will, He heareth us: and if we know that He hear us, whatsoever we ask, we know that we have the petitions that we desired of Him."

1 John 5:14-15

The apostle Paul prayed to God to have a thorn removed from his flesh, but God did not remove it.

God chose otherwise, because what Paul prayed concerning the thorn that was in his flesh, was not according to God's will. Even though the Apostle was the lone disciple who received so much revelation from God that he was able to write 13 of the 27 books of the New Testament, he still did not know the will of God at that point in time when he asked that petition of God. At the end, we see Paul turn his will over to God as he realized that God always knows best.

"And lest I should be exalted above measure through the abundance of the revelations, there was given to me a thorn in the flesh, the messenger of Satan to buffet me, lest I should be exalted above measure. For this thing I besought the Lord thrice, that it might depart from me. And he said unto me, My grace is sufficient for thee: for my strength is made perfect in weakness. Most gladly therefore will I rather glory in my infirmities, that the power of Christ may rest upon me."

2 Cor. 12:7-9

When Jesus faced the most difficult hour of His earthly life, He began to pray, and ask His Father if He would keep Him from going through this hard thing He was faced with, *"Saying Father, if Thou be* willing, remove this cup from me: nevertheless not My will, but Thine, be done. And there appeared an angel unto Him from heaven, strengthening Him" (Luke 22:42-43).

Jesus knew the will of the Father, and He also knew what He was sent here to do, that's the reason He immediately recanted before the words of prayer left His mouth, by saying, "Nevertheless not my will, but Thine, be done."

Sin in Ones Life

From the beginning, sin has been the separator that placed a divide between God and humans. When Jesus went to the cross, He took upon Himself the sins of the world and became sin for us. Because God despises sin, as His only begotten Son hung dying, He could not look upon Him. After Jesus died upon the cross, and then subsequently had to go to hell; a bridge was put in place that reconnected God to His creation in a different way.

"The LORD is far from the wicked: but He [hears] the prayer of the righteous."

Prov. 15:29

The following is a list of Scriptures, where you find the heart of God concerning His decision not to answer the prayers of believers who regard iniquity in their hearts:

- Psalms 34:15-16
- Psalms 66:18
- Proverbs 15:29
- Isaiah 59:1-2
- 1Peter 3:12

Does God hear a sinner's prayers? This is one of those questions that for centuries, has been the subject matter of many a debate. For those who believe that the only prayer God hears from sinners is a prayer of repentance, this is the Scripture they use, *"Now we know that God heareth not sinners: but if any man be a worshipper of God, and doeth His will, him He heareth"* (John 9:31).

For those who believe that there were very few occasions in which God heard a prayer prayed by a sinner, and it were not a prayer of repentance, but of faith, they use these Scriptures: Mark 7:25-30 (the Syrophenician woman); Mark 10:46 (Blind Bartimaeus); 2 Chronicles 33:12-13 (Evil King Manasseh). One never knows God's plans, as

He may by chance, hearken to the voice of someone that is doing evil in His sight. Intercession may have gone up on their behalf, or by performing a miracle, God gets the glory from it, causing many others to come into His Kingdom. God has a universal plan that must ultimately come to pass. Should we sin that grace may abound? God forbid. The Word of God makes no provisions for living in sin. We must never rely completely on God's mercy, but on His Word, which will never fail.

Ask Amiss

"Ye ask, and receive not, because ye ask amiss, that ye may consume it upon your lusts."

James 4:3

Prayers that are prayed amiss are prayers in which someone asks for a particular thing, or a plethora of things, in lust, thinking that the multiplicity of things would bring them some kind of glory, or worldly status.

A person may ask for a new car, so they can cruise up to the church and have everyone admire them, believing that because of things; they are blessed. They ask for a new home, not so they can possess the land as God desires, but they ask so they can be the best on their block. They ask for a promotion in the church, so they can sit on the platform glamorously, and have everyone admire their prestige.

Hunger for *things*, which is brought about by a worldly appetite, causes one to pray for worldly things. In order to satisfy that hunger, one will eventually be led in the wrong direction, pursuing carnal and ungodly things. So asking amiss is asking incorrectly, or inappropriately, and God will not answer prayers that are prayed with perverse motives.

Pure Unadulterated Unbelief

When the term "unadulterated" is used to describe unbelief, it is saying that unbelief, in this case, is absolute. A person simply does not believe, period! That settles it, and there is nothing else that can be said which would cause that person to have an inkling of faith.

On occasion, people can have a desire to obtain things from God; but will stand in a fraction, not total, but a fraction of doubt and unbelief. There is a case cited in Scripture when a father, whose son was possessed with a demon, came to Jesus to have his son delivered. *"Jesus said unto him, If thou canst believe, all things are possible to him that believeth. And straightway the father of the child cried out, and said with tears, Lord, I believe; help Thou mine unbelief"* (Mark 9:23-24).

In Mark 5:35-43, there lies an account where the daughter of the ruler of the synagogue was dead, and Jesus was entreated to come and heal her. Upon entering the house, and saying that the little girl was not dead, only asleep, everyone there laughed Him to scorn.

In order for miracles and healings to take place, the atmosphere has to be seasoned with faith. When Jesus was attempting to heal this little girl, He had to send everyone out of the place, except for the father, mother, and the disciples who came along with Him, because of the doubt they held. When all of the doubt and unbelief was expelled, Jesus could then, and only then, bring about the miracle that was needed for the little girl, and her parents.

Abraham also held a fraction of doubt, in that he produced a child by another woman before the promised child was conceived, but he still held some faith, and believed God. Then it was imputed unto him as righteousness, and he was the recipient of the promise made to him by God.

"He staggered not at the promise of God through unbelief; but was strong in faith, giving glory to God."

Rom. 4:20

A Prophet is Without Honor

"And he did not many mighty works there because of their unbelief."

Matt. 13:58

Scripture says that Jesus Himself, could not do many miracles in His country, because He was among the people He grew up with, and they were too familiar with Him. "A prophet is without honor in His own Country," is a statement of fact proven by the life of Jesus. The people there knew Jesus as the son of Mary, and Joseph the carpenter. If you go where everybody knows you, from your childhood up, it is hard to get that particular people to see past what they knew you to be before God came into your life.

Have you ever wondered why so many more miracles of healings and deliverances take place seemingly without limits, on the backside of third world countries? I have come to the realization that those who have never heard the *good news* of the Gospel preached are eager to hear, and accept it. And along with the "Good News," they receive the messenger that was sent to bring it.

Need for Prayer and Fasting

"Howbeit this kind [goes] not out but by prayer and fasting."

Matt. 17:21

There are some difficulties we face that call for intensified prayer, and along with that, "fasting," in order to destroy the demonic hold the enemy has over our life. In fasting, we die out to our flesh, as our spirits become more alive unto God. When the spirit is strong, then faith is strong, when faith is strong, our resolve is strong, when our resolve is strong we will hold on until we see the desired end of the matter.

.

Chapter 9

An Open Line for Prayer

Scripture encourages us to pray without ceasing. How is that possible? Am I to assume that one must stay on their knees praying to God; hour after hour, day in and day out, all the time? The answer is "No." That is virtually impossible. We must be afforded opportunity to live life. If we incorporate prayer into our life by thinking of prayer as a total consciousness of God at all times, instead of an activity we complete before running off to attend to our life situations, then we would know that there is always an open line for prayer.

"Pray without ceasing."

1 Thess. 5:17

> *"Prayer should be looked at as a 'way of life,' and not something that gets in the way of life."*
> —Mary Simpson—

How Long Should We Pray

Where did the idea or notion of praying for one hour originate?

When Jesus went up to pray, and upon His return, He found His disciples asleep, He asked them, *"What, could [you] not watch with Me one Hour"* (Matt. 26:40-41).

We find that the idea originated centuries ago with the Romans, and has since crept into Christianity. The early Jews prayed three times a day. The most important hours were the third and ninth. The third hour (believed to be instituted by Abraham), the sixth hour (instituted by Isaac), and ninth hour (instituted by Jacob), were the times they set aside for prayer. Those hours are the same as our 9 in the morning, 12 noon, and 3 in the afternoon.

David said in Ps. 55:17, that he prayed during

the evening, morning, and noon time. Daniel told of how many times he was accustomed to pray in Dan. 6:10. In Acts 2:15, they prayed at the third hour, in Acts 10:9, they prayed at the sixth hour, and in Acts 3:1, mention is made of the ninth hour of prayer.

Direct reference is made in Scripture to the times, not duration of prayers. Indications about the length of prayers were made earlier on in this writing. It is not my conviction that it is necessary to set a length of time for prayer. One might pray thirty minutes, one hour, or one hour thirty minutes. When you are finished, you are finished. There is no need to waste time waiting for the clock to alarm, indicating that your hour is up, and you are now free to leave.

Upon thorough study by theologians throughout history, no set length of time to pray has been found in Scripture, and they are reluctant to say that there is an instructed duration of time we should adhere to. But, most of them believe, as I do, that one hour is sufficient as a *minimum* time to set aside for communion with God. One-half hour should be spent for actual verbal expression to God, and the other one-half hour should be spent in the Word, desiring to hear back from Him.

I am convinced that if we as The Church would become liberal enough to take some of the human mandates off of prayer, people will be more apt to enter into its sanctity. I believe the questions of time, duration of time, posture, list, or no list, and etc., exudes a negative connotation about prayer. If we teach believers to enter the presence of God with praise upon their lips, faith in their hearts, vision in their spiritual eyes, and a determination down on the inside, they will view prayer in a much different way. God has placed in order the things He deems necessary on how Christians should meet Him in prayer; because He knows that ultimately, sincere and fervent words which are spoken from the depths of the heart, is the key!

A Set Time and Place for Prayer

After Jesus died upon the cross, and the veil was rent from top to bottom, that blessed event opened up access to the presence of God at any place, anytime, and by any Christian, not just priest. Yes, we can pray to God anytime and anywhere, but it would be preferable to have a specific time and place set aside for communion with the Father. If you dare promise to meet God at a special time and place, say your prayer closet or prayer room, it is my personal promise to you, "He will meet you there every time." The atmosphere will have already been set; so when you enter, you enter into the presence of God, because He will be there waiting, anticipating your arrival. If we do not set aside a regular time for prayer, we, in our humanness, will probably forget.

People of all faiths have practiced praying at certain times and places. *Acts 3:1 states: "Now Peter and John went up together into the temple at the hour of prayer, being the ninth hour."*

My place of communion with my Father is found in this excerpt from **Dew Drops From Heaven,** which is a sequel to this book.

"There is a pivotal point where the darkness of night transcends into the glorious dawning of a new day. You are there, suspended between two peripheral points, not quite awakened out of your sleep, and not yet awakened unto your day. Realization of what's happening around you has not come into focus. Thoughts of what your day will bring have not yet begun to flood in. You are primed for the voice of God to begin speaking with you. Your spirit man is awakening unto God, but your soulish man has not

fully awakened to your surroundings.

It is this author's humble belief, that God, in His infinite wisdom, has reserved a place in our day that is just for Himself; a place where He can minister unto His children, when they are fresh, and able to hear His voice uninhibited. In that poised moment, He begins to rain down dew drops of wisdom from the throne room of heaven—drip, drip, drip—ever so gently upon our brow. This wisdom would make our day a success, if we were to attend unto His voice.

Some of us are disturbed out of our sleep, by the annoying sound of an alarm clock. Others are awakened by the caring arms of a loved one we cherish so dear. Many of us are roused by the patter of little feet, on their way to get something to eat. The ring-ring-ring of a phone may startle some of us out of our sleep. But, oh how sweet it is, to be awakened by the loving touch of our Father from up above."

On the right side of my bed, somewhere between the hours of 4 and 6 o'clock a.m., is the time and place I meet with *my* Father, from up above. Many a revelation has been given and received *right there*, during those early, early morning hours.

I find myself going to bed each night, in great anticipation of awakening the next morning, bask-ing in the glory of God's presence. It is during those early morning hours that my mind and spirit are the most alert, and open to receive from Him.

As I finish this work, I leave with you these words of wisdom, "Yes, set aside a time and place to meet with your Heavenly Father, then He will meet you there, and not disappoint."

Pray, pray, and pray again!

Pray There Before You Get There!

Pray There Before You Get There

About Your Author

Mary is a Christian author who possesses much wisdom and knowledge of God's word. She has been saved and walking with God for over 33 years. Within those years, she has acquired experience, understanding, insight and astuteness in and of God's Word. One main artery of learning for her was the school of Ministry at Heritage Christian Center in Denver, Colorado. She possesses 33 years of devout study in numerous venues of biblical studies.

Mary is a licensed and ordained minister of the Gospel, as well as a Board Certified Pastoral Counselor serving at Emmanuel Christian Center. She has accepted her call to write and put into words the heart of God as she understands it.

This is Mary's second book. Her first book was a mini book entitled *The Art of Compromise*, which was written as a help to her and her husband as they teach marriage enhancement classes together. She has another major book being released in mid 2008, entitled: *In Pursuit of God's Presence: The Ultimate Quest*, which can be found online or in bookstores near you.

Mary has been happily married to her husband "Will" for over 32 years. They live in Denver, Colorado and are the proud parents of three adult children, and two beautiful grandbabies.

PRAY THERE BEFORE YOU GET THERE

Future Releases

If this work has been a blessing to you, look for these exciting future projects, soon to be released by Mary Simpson.

Other books coming soon are entitled:

Dew Drops From Heaven
Release Date pending
Published by Marriage Connection

In Pursuit of God's Presence
The Ultimate Quest, *release date: April 24, 2008*
Published by Xulon Press
ISBN no. 9781604779219

Prayer Notes

Prayer Notes

Prayer Notes